HAMTRAMCK
THROUGH THE YEARS

HAMTRAMCK
THROUGH THE YEARS

Greg Kowalski

THE
History
PRESS

Published by The History Press
Charleston, SC
www.historypress.com

All images courtesy of the Hamtramck Historical Society.

First published 2023

Manufactured in the United States

ISBN 9781467153713

Library of Congress Control Number: 2023932162

This is dedicated to all the people of Hamtramck, past and present.

CONTENTS

ACKNOWLEDGEMENTS

This book would have been nearly impossible to create without access to the Hamtramck Historical Museum archives. They are a treasure house of information.

INTRODUCTION

Step into the past…

Take your pick of a time and place and try to imagine what life was like then and there. It isn't easy. No matter how good your imagination is, it seems like you can't truly capture the past. There are just too many details that will be missed. Photos are helpful. They depict scenes untainted by emotion and are not subject to failed memories, misconceptions and inaccuracies that have been around for so long they are accepted as facts. But what about the sounds and smells of the past? Recordings help to an extent, but recorded voices are limited to barely more than a century. And the wonderful memory of mom's cooking can never be accurately related to someone else.

So can we truly experience the past? Not entirely, but it is possible to get a sense of what life was like in a certain time and place by tapping into the sources of the time. Letters, personal diaries, newspaper stories and myriad other documents can enhance the historical facts that make up the details of somewhere years ago. Like mosaic pieces, they collectively form a picture. In some cases, memories of those still living can give us a clearer view.

What matters, however, is that a detailed image is created. Too many historical recounts are antiseptic or, worse, superficial. They are heavy on drama but lacking details. And it's the details that make the difference. They make a story something we can relate to. They provide the links that allow us to connect to the person, place or event, and once that connection is made, history comes alive.

Hamtramck, Michigan, is a city with an incredible history. It started as a massive township formed in 1798. Originally, it stretched from Base Line (Eight Mile Road) to the Detroit River and from near Woodward Avenue to Lake St. Clair. It was named in honor of a French Canadian, Jean François (later legally changed to John Francis) Hamtramck, who came to fight with the fledgling American army in the Revolutionary War. It was troops under his command who finally took Detroit out of the hands of the British on the orders of President George Washington in 1796. Throughout the nineteenth century, Hamtramck Township shrank as the city of Detroit grew and annexed portions of Hamtramck bit by bit. In 1900, a group of residents living in the area that makes up Hamtramck today decided they did not want to be Detroiters and formed the Village of Hamtramck. The village, covering roughly 2.1 square miles, was officially created in 1901. It was a sleepy little farming town, hardly more than a bump in the road between Detroit and not much else. Most of the residents were German immigrant farmers who also operated some popular stores and saloons.

That all changed in 1909 when John and Horace Dodge drove into town. The Dodge brothers built parts for Henry Ford, who had just opened a large plant in the neighboring town of Highland Park. But the Dodges had their own plans. They wanted to build cars, too, and compete with Ford. So they came to Hamtramck, where the taxes were lower and there was plenty of space to grow.

In September 1909, they bought a piece of land in the south end of Hamtramck, and by the end of 1910, factory buildings had been erected and manufacturing had begun. Even then they had bigger plans. But for the Dodge plant to expand, it needed workers. The Dodge brothers put out a call that was answered in a huge way. Hordes of immigrants, mainly Polish, flooded into Hamtramck. In 1910, there were about 3,500 people living in the 2.1-square-mile village. In 1920, Hamtramck had 48,000 residents. The growth was staggering and fairly unmanageable. Yet somehow the town survived and thrived. By the late teen years of the twentieth century, the Poles vastly outnumbered the earlier German settlers, and in 1922, the Village of Hamtramck incorporated as the City of Hamtramck. The Poles engineered the change so that a new government would be formed and give them a chance to gain power. Within two years, Poles achieved their goal, as they took almost complete political control of the city.

Hamtramck's population peaked at fifty-six thousand in 1930 and declined thereafter. The city was just too crowded. The slow decline continued into the 1990s, when Hamtramck's population dipped to about eighteen thousand. But the 2000 census revealed something remarkable: Hamtramck's population had grown to twenty-four thousand. A somewhat stunned city administration dove into the figures and learned that Hamtramck was undergoing a new immigrant influx; only this time, the newcomers were arriving from a host of countries. That growth has continued unbroken since then, and Hamtramck is now one of the most diverse cities in the nation.

This story is actually hundreds of thousands of stories. At least. Each is unique, yet all are related. On these pages, we will explore a handful of people and what they experienced in intricate detail with the intent of giving a real sense of what they would have felt. The pivotal characters who anchor some chapter are fictional but actually not. They are compilations of many people whose experiences are drawn together to create a cohesive, encompassing, accurate portrait of life in their time. The events, places and details are authentic and as accurate as can be re-created.

So step into the past in these pages and get a taste (and smell and sound) of what life was really like here in times gone by and how Hamtramck came to be what it is today.

1

1890

I t started at the river.

In July 1701, Antoine de la Mothe Cadillac, with his troop of one hundred men, disembarked after passing through the narrowing of the river. Something earlier caught his attention, although it took a day for him to act on it. After spending the night farther downriver and camping on a large island, he went back to the area where high bluffs lined the river, which was barely a half-mile wide at this point.

This is it, he thought. This was the best place to establish a new settlement. So construction began on Fort Pontchartrain. And the city of Detroit was born.

This was still nearly a century before Hamtramck Township formed, but the foundation was in place, and from it would grow the range of communities that would shape southeast Michigan, including Hamtramck.

That probably never entered Cadillac's mind as he stood on the shore of the river. You can still get a sense of the modest majesty of the area by standing at the tip of Belle Isle. Look toward the Detroit skyline. In Cadillac's time, there were great stands of oaks, elms, pines and other trees stretching into the background. Today, the steep bluffs are gone, although you can still feel the dip as Woodward Avenue ends at Hart Plaza, which falls down to the riverfront. Now, the Ambassador Bridge draws a distant line across the river. Massive ships pass underneath at a regular rate. It's more urban in a way that Cadillac could never have imagined, but some things have remained the same. The wind still blows strong across the waves, and a July sunset can

Antoine de la Mothe Cadillac is immortalized at Hart Place, just a short distance from where he landed on the bank of the Detroit River in 1701. The site became the city of Detroit.

be a golden miracle of subtle colors. It doesn't seem as though Cadillac was a man who would appreciate the charm of a peaceful sunset. He got into a lot of trouble in later years for selling alcohol to the Indians and supposedly abusing power. Shades of things to come: alcohol and power would become a recurring theme in the history of Hamtramck.

Cadillac was French, of course, and had made his way to *le detroit*, "the strait," from Montreal and ushered in the period when the French dominated Detroit as it gradually grew north up from the river. Settlers began buying property from the Indians in a dubious process that later raised a lot of questions as to the legitimacy of such transactions. Further, Cadillac and other officials began making land grants to individuals that also ended up being challenged for legitimacy. Even so, the number of farms, mainly strung alongside the river, grew. Most were narrow and deep, extending north into the wilderness. These "ribbon farms" were designed to allow more people to have access to the river. Also, because the lots were narrow, there was less distance between the houses on them. This was a safety consideration, as the early settlers were still subject to Indian attacks. That threat faded as development of the city continued.

The farm of Louis Chapoton was typical. It was four arpents wide by thirty-six arpents deep. An arpent is a French unit of land measurement equal to about 0.85 of an acre. Chapoton had a cow and two horses. Jacques Laintaubin's farm was two arpents wide by forty deep, and he had two horses. In general, the house was close to the river at the front of the lot. A garden would be nearby, with an orchard behind that. Farther back would be fields of wheat and corn.

Life on the frontier was harsh. Whims of the weather could mean crop failure; attacks by Indians were a threat in the early years, and there was growing friction between the French and British. The fort provided some sense of security, but it was small, and with each farm pushing farther from it, the sense of isolation would grow. Jefferson Avenue was the main road and linked the farms, but it was an era long before streetlights, telephones, streetcars and even railroads.

Nights were dark. No, not that shade of gray that passes for nighttime in the city now. This was wilderness dark, when the Milky Way was clearly visible looping across the sky. There were thousands of stars glowing with an intensity that faded into the city lights in the coming decades as Detroit developed. At the riverside, the splashes of unseen creatures diving into the water could be heard. And the geese and gulls squawked then as they do today. Both types of birds still have an arrogance that they demonstrate when mere humans intrude on their space.

On a calm summer night, the scene would have been serene. But winters were as fierce as the summers were mild. Wood was cut and collected in prodigious amounts to fuel fireplaces in the modest early homes. Ironically, that situation would hardly improve for nearly two centuries, as into the

1900s, the houses of the immigrants in Hamtramck were being heated with coal-burning stoves and furnaces. But just as with the later immigrants, the early settlers survived, though not without difficulty. While some harvests were plentiful, others were not. In 1714, the farmers were able to export 2,400 bushels of corn from Detroit. But by 1747, conditions had deteriorated so badly that the people sought aid from Montreal. A convoy of 150 persons was sent with food to rescue the settlers and save them from starvation. When times were better, the settlers had a variety of food, including fish, corn, wheat and even beavers. Fruit, especially cherries and apples, was plentiful. Pears were a favorite, too, and almost every farm had a stand of pear trees, which may have been used to mark property boundaries. The pear trees were so popular, legends sprang up about them. One related that a young French teacher was given a pear by his soon-to-be bride, who suddenly died just before they were married. The story goes on that he was assigned to teach at the settlement at Detroit and brought the pear with him. The man was still grief-stricken, and a priest here told him to plant the pear "to bless mankind." Nice story, but the seeds for the trees were likely brought over from France by settlers. For a long time, the pear trees were a defining element of the Detroit landscape. Some other things were special to this area, such as maple sugar. The sweetener was so popular that 150,000 pounds of maple sugar were produced in 1819 in Michigan. Maple sugar could be used for cooking or as a special treat on its own. Indian children were especially fond of it. The farmers also

The Native American Indians harvested wild corn before the early European settlers drained the marshes in the Detroit area. This scene is part of the *Coming to Hamtramck* mural by artist Dennis Orlowski and is in the Hamtramck Historical Museum.

had an abundance of cattle, and there was plenty of pastureland for them to roam after the area wetlands had been drained by early settlers. This transformation of the landscape also resulted in the end of harvesting wild rice, which the Indians did before the arrival of Europeans.

Fish were plentiful. Perch, bass, pike, catfish and sturgeon were popular. Yet food shortages persisted. Further severe shortages were experienced in 1770 and 1780, years after the British had taken control of the Detroit area on November 29, 1760, during the French and Indian War.

But seemingly, conditions remained unstable. On March 10, 1780, Arent Schuyler DePeyster, commandant of Fort Detroit, wrote to the commandant at Fort Niagara that "the distress of the inhabitants here is very great for want of bread, not an ounce of flour or a grain of corn to be purchased." Famine wasn't the only threat. In 1752, smallpox broke out, killing eighty Indians in villages near Detroit, and other diseases, including typhoid and cholera, would periodically strike well into the nineteenth century.

Despite those threats, the settlement continued to grow, and by the early 1760s, some forty births were being recorded yearly in the community. Although there was a dip in the numbers in 1764, when many settlers left Detroit to go to the then newly founded St. Louis, the population continued to grow. In 1778, a census of Detroit showed a population of 564 men, 274 women, 530 young men and boys, 172 male servants, 39 female servants and 127 slaves. Along with the people, 885 cows, 470 sheep and 1,312 hogs were counted.

Those were the domesticated animals. Just behind the back fences and fields, a wide array of wild animals roamed. Elk, moose, wolves, rabbits, lynxes, beavers, muskrats and bears prowled through the underbrush or swam in the lakes, ponds, creeks and rivers that defined the landscape. Overhead, wild pigeons flew in vast numbers and turkeys trotted across the countryside. But the bears may have been the most concerning. They certainly were a threat well into the nineteenth century. A bear, in fact, was responsible for one of the most notorious tragedies in Hamtramck's history.

According to a story that originated in the *Detroit Free Press* newspaper in 1857 and drew national attention, there was a fatal bear attack that horrified the community and appeared to shock people as much back then as it would if such a thing occurred today. The headline stated it well: "Dreadful Occurrence—A Boy Eaten Up by a Bear, Almost Within City Limits." The story related that Joseph Rademacher went berry picking with his brother in the wilds of Hamtramck "some five or six miles out."

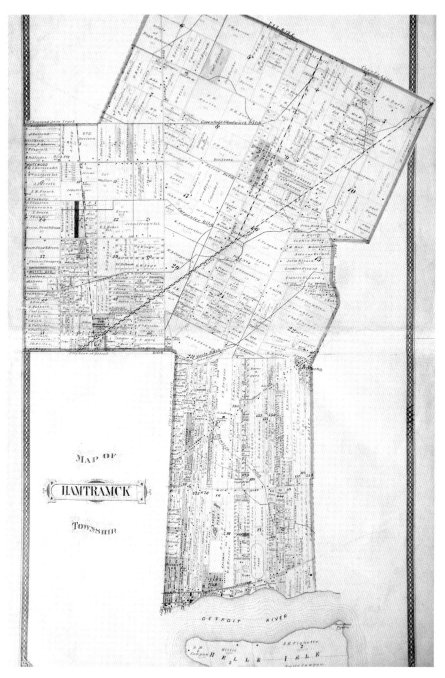

Hamtramck Township had already lost the Grosse Pointes, which split off to form separate communities in 1848, when this map was prepared in 1874. Woodward Avenue (roughly) is at left, Base Line (Eight Mile Road) is at top, the Detroit River is at bottom and the Grosse Pointes at right.

By this time, Hamtramck Township had been formed. It was a vast expanse that extended up from the Detroit River to Base Line, which is now known in these parts as Eight Mile Road. If the boys did go "five or six miles" in a straight line up from the river, that would have put them in the area Hamtramck is now. But they may have followed a more winding path and were closer to the Detroit city limits, which were much nearer to the downtown area then. In any case, the paper described them as going into the "marshes of Hamtramck."

After several hours of berry picking, they stopped to have lunch. Before they realized it, a female bear and three cubs appeared and took their lunch baskets. The boys fled, and this is where the story takes a tragic turn.

As the two boys were racing from the bears, they nearly ran into two other boys, ages eleven and thirteen, who had no idea there was a bear nearby. The paper picks up the story:

> *Rademacher saw two boys not far from him when he left the spot, but said nothing to them. Before* [he and] *his brother had got a safe distance they heard terrible screams in the direction they had left, which only served to accelerate their pace, and place a greater distance between themselves and danger. They were soon overtaken by one of the boys, who came rushing up bewildered with fright, screaming that the bear was eating up his brother. Rademacher received this intelligence in utter dismay, and took to his heels with a will followed by the two boys and deserted the sufferer to his fate.*

The three stumbled to the city, where they raised an alarm. A rescue party was quickly formed, which set out into the countryside, where they found the grisly scene. The bear had eaten half of the eleven-year-old boy and buried the rest "for a future meal."

"Remnants of clothes were scattered around, together with a coat, torn to pieces," the paper related. But there was no sign of the bear, which was never caught.

The surviving boy said that he and his brother came upon the bear without warning. The bear turned, growled at them and then grabbed his little brother.

The paper was not kind toward Rademacher: "A word of warning from Rademacher when he commenced his flight would have saved the boy, but he was too frightened to do anything but run."

There was equal outrage over such a thing even happening. "The contemplation of such an occurrence, happening almost within the limits of a city of 70,000 inhabitants is sickening and terrible," the paper said.

"Wild bears have become a rarity in most parts of the state, yet we are visited in the very metropolis by one that perpetuates a deed that belongs only to the early annals of our history. It is hoped that such visits will be rare in the future."

They were more than rare, as there are no other known reports of bear attacks in Hamtramck.

Confrontations with humans, however, were more common. One of the earliest and worst occurred in 1763. The French and Indian War had just ended, and the British were in control. They had a bad relationship with the local Indians, particularly Chief Pontiac, who had formed a consortium to drive the British out of the area and laid siege to Fort Detroit (the later renamed Fort Pontchartrain). On July 31, 250 soldiers from the fort attempted to attack Pontiac's encampment outside of Detroit. But Pontiac had been warned, possibly by French settlers who also opposed the British. Pontiac's warriors surprised the British soldiers at Parent's Creek, about two miles from Fort Detroit. In the ensuing battle, about twenty British soldiers were killed and more than thirty wounded. There supposedly was so much blood the water in the creek ran red. And so it became known as Bloody Run. *Run* is another word for "creek." The commander of the fort, Captain James Dalyell, was killed in the attack. The surviving soldiers made their way back to the fort, which remained under siege until October, when the attack just faded away. The British held control of the area until well after the Revolutionary War.

So where was Hamtramck during all of this excitement?

Hamtramck the town was still years away in the future. Hamtramck the man was a youngster when the Battle of Bloody Run occurred. Jean François Hamtramck was born on August 14, 1756, the son of Charles David Hamtramck and Marie-Anne Bertin, who had married in 1753. Hamtramck came to Quebec, Canada, from what is now Luxembourg in 1749 and was a barber. During the French and Indian War, Quebec was taken over by the British in 1759 and was ceded to the British as part of the Treaty of Paris, which ended the war. It isn't clear what Hamtramck experienced in this time, but in 1775, he enlisted in the American army, beginning a long career in the military, extending well beyond the Revolutionary War. Along that route, he changed his name to John Francis. Following the Revolutionary War, the British had refused to leave Detroit, and the army was not strong enough to drive them out until 1796, when President George Washington sent General

Anthony Wayne and Colonel Hamtramck to Detroit to force the British to leave. By then, Hamtramck had reached the rank of colonel, and his troops had no difficulty convincing the British to leave. Hamtramck settled in Detroit and had a cabin built on the shore of the Detroit River, next to what is now Fr. Gabriel Richard Park, which itself is next to the Belle Isle bridge.

Colonel Hamtramck died in 1803 and was buried in the cemetery at St. Anne's Church in Detroit. His body was later moved to Mt. Elliott Cemetery, not far from Bloody Run, and moved again, in 1962, to the city of Hamtramck, where he now rests.

Hamtramck, the town, appeared on maps in 1798 when the first iteration of Hamtramck Township was created. It encompassed a vast area stretching from Base Line (the north county line, which is now Eight Mile Road) on the north to the Detroit River on the south and from roughly Woodward Avenue on the west to Lake St. Clair on the east. Almost immediately, Detroit began annexing pieces of the township. It wasn't a complete land grab. In 1909, a group of Hamtramck Township residents living near Gratiot Avenue in what is now central Detroit petitioned the city to annex their neighborhood. The problem was that it was filthy. Open ditches filled with sewage were common, and aside from the smell, they were breeding grounds for diseases, including typhoid fever and cholera.

"We had nine weeks of typhoid fever in our family, and there was nothing to blame for it except our bad drainage," a resident told a Detroit committee meeting called to consider annexation.

"My cellar smells worse than the ditch outside," said another. They were among a group of residents who urged the Detroit officials to annex the area. All said they needed better sanitation and were willing to pay higher taxes to get it. Detroit had the resources to install sewer and water lines. Ultimately, Detroit obliged them.

Early Hamtramck roads were clustered near the Detroit River. The cost of maintaining the roads was covered by an elaborate scale of tolls that ranged from three-quarters of a cent for each animal after three drawing a wagon to two cents for vehicles drawn by two animals.

Hamtramck Township already had a reputation as an uninviting place to settle. It was swampy, wild and remote. In an era when there were few roads, if any, this was especially important because carts pulled by oxen could not travel through the boggy soil, limiting movement. A person just trying to walk through the underbrush would find it difficult. Yet growth was inevitable. While the early settlers found the riverside more welcoming, it provided a limited amount of space. After the fire of 1805, and with the rebuilding of Detroit, it was necessary for more people to move farther inland, especially as the riverside became more industrialized. Docks, warehouses, grain elevators, rail lines and yards and factories took up an increasing amount of space. The waterfront was fast losing its wilderness character as it became urbanized and industrialized.

In 1818, when Wayne County was formed in southeastern Michigan, Hamtramck Township was restructured. Already, portions of the township had been annexed by Detroit, and in 1827, a third and final iteration of Hamtramck Township was defined. Through the nineteenth century, Detroit grew. Its population stood at 1,422 in 1820; 21,019 in 1850; and 205,876 in 1890. Hamtramck Township recorded 1,063 residents in 1827 and 5,657 in 1884. Despite the difficulties of homesteading, by 1884, there were 152 farms listed in Hamtramck.

In the 1830s, the railroads came to Michigan. The Detroit and St. Joseph Railroad was among the first to roll into town. It ran across the southern part of the state to St. Joseph on Lake Michigan. A key rail for Hamtramck was the Detroit and Pontiac Railroad, which was formed in 1838. It ran from Detroit north to Royal Oak. Although initially the rail cars were drawn by horses, they were soon propelled by steam locomotives—which traveled at a whopping ten miles per hour.

But they did connect Detroit to the new suburbs growing north of Detroit. Also, more roads began pushing up away from Detroit. Woodward Avenue was soon joined by a tangle of roads, including Chene, St. Aubin, Dequindre and Conant. These streets still exist and have become the main arteries connecting present-day Hamtramck to Detroit and beyond.

It isn't clear why or how the area occupied by the present city of Hamtramck developed as opposed to some other part of the township. Jos. Campau Avenue likely played a role, as it was a main artery through the area from its earliest days. The rail lines, too, made this a traffic hub and would make it extremely attractive to industries. And oddly, one of the most distinguishing features of early Hamtramck was the Beth-olem Cemetery. The 2.2-acre site was bought by two of Detroit's Jewish residents in 1862. But the first burial

RES.& GREEN HOUSES OF **ALBERT BREITMEYER**, HAMTRAMCK, WAYNE Co., MICH.

The Breitmeyer farm was located in Hamtramck Township near where Ellery Street just west of Mt. Elliott Street is today. In the late nineteenth century, this area was mainly farmland. Ironically, after rapid development in the early twentieth century, the area has been largely abandoned and is now reverting to its original wild state.

wasn't recorded until 1871. At the time, the cemetery was fairly remote, and the dead rested in serene countryside. But that wouldn't last long as the area developed in the twentieth century, and factory smokestacks replaced the trees. There were two synagogues in Hamtramck, one at the cemetery and one at the end of Wyandotte Street, but in the early 1920s, what few Jewish people who were here moved to western Detroit and beyond. The last burial at Beth-olem was in 1948, and about 1,100 people are interred there. All were at risk of being moved when General Motors built its giant factory nearby in the early 1980s, but ultimately it was decided to leave the cemetery alone. Today it stands peacefully protected on the grounds of the factory. It is open to the public on two Jewish holidays during the year.

Other than that, there was little to make this area stand out in the late nineteenth century. It is situated about five miles north of the Detroit River and roughly three miles from the county line. Further, it was not a particularly appealing area. The landscape was swampy, and as late as the 1960s, a swamp existed at the point where Caniff Street merges into Mt. Elliott Street just beyond the eastern edge of Hamtramck. This site is now occupied by a supermarket and a Detroit Edison Company substation. The area was also crossed by several creeks, including Holbrook Creek and Carpenter Creek.

The Dickinson farm, north of Holbrook Creek and east of Jos. Campau Avenue, later became the site of Dickinson East Elementary School, which serves the community today.

There are also map references to a creek that ran roughly along Commor Street on Hamtramck's north side, and there are accounts of a large pond on Conant Avenue where Our Lady Queen of Apostles Church stands today. During the winter, the pond would freeze over and people would skate there.

Those railroads and streets surely were a lure to the growing cadre of industrialists who saw opportunities in this area of Hamtramck Township. They would, in fact, be the routes leading to the future of Hamtramck's industrial nature. One of the earliest Hamtramck industrialists was George H. Russel, who established the Hamtramck Iron Works in Hamtramck Township in the 1850s. It was located at the foot of Meldrum Street on the Detroit River, next to where Mt. Elliott Park is today. Family members also would go on to create the Russel Wheel & Foundry in what later would become the village of Hamtramck. This was a first step in the evolution of Hamtramck from a farming community to an industrial one. And it did not bode well.

Working in the factory was dangerous, even for the owners. At one point, possibly in the 1880s—the date isn't clear—George H. Russel's father, George B. Russel, became seriously ill. In a letter, George H.'s wife, Annie Davenport Russel, noted her father-in-law was sick with a "congestive chill": "He was much alarmed. He spit up blood for several days but seems almost well again. He was about the foundry and watching men dig and clean up and thinks malaria the cause of his sickness and it was cold and damp in the old shops."

The Russels, who operated their business in Hamtramck into the early twentieth century, weren't the only industrialists who played an early role in the Hamtramck we know today, though it wasn't even a village yet. In the 1890s, William L. Davis and Thomas Neal, founders of the Acme White Lead Paint Company, relocated their operations from the west side of Detroit to a site next to the railroad tracks along St. Aubin Street in Hamtramck. This would grow into a major operation and helped reinforce Hamtramck's increasing status as an industrial hub.

So what was life like for the average Hamtramckan then? Generally tough. Most Hamtramckans worked on farms, where they made an average of about $23 a month. Factory workers fared better, making about $50 a month, but often worked horrendous hours and often seven days a week. Skilled professionals could do better. Harry Russel, of the iron foundry, left the family business to be attorney for the Michigan Central Railroad for $150 a month.

Prices, of course, were lower. On average, flour was $0.05 a pound, coffee was $0.19 a pound, sugar $0.10 a pound, rice $0.10 a pound and dried cod fish was $0.08 a pound if it was available locally. Beef was $0.17 a pound,

By the 1960s, this house on Clay Street was ready to be demolished. It likely was built in the 1880s. Note the lack of shingles and gutters and clapboard siding. This is one of the oldest areas of Hamtramck.

I.E. Jozefiak was one of the businesses that provided the necessities of life in Hamtramck, including coal, coke and wood to use in stoves in the home.

veal $0.20, ham $0.15, pork $0.13 and cheese $0.18 a pound. Eggs were $0.40 a dozen. Coal, mainly used to heat a home, was $7.84 a ton.

Truly, in that time, every penny counted. But life wasn't entirely grim. People found ways to be entertained without screens to stare at. As Detroit historian Thomas W. Palmer noted in his delightful *Detroit in 1837* pamphlet, "We had no furnace, hot water heaters, nor steam, only some crude stoves, open fireplaces and the Franklin [stove]; no gas, only tallow candles and lamps and sperm candles for company, but the ladies dressed just as tastefully, if not as extravagantly then as now, and the men were a little more gallant."

And there were special activities. As late as 1857, the Michigan State Fair was held in Hamtramck Township, and the Detroit Driving Club (horse racetrack) was a popular attraction alongside Jefferson Avenue near Van Dyke Avenue. It operated there from the 1850s to the 1890s before moving to the Grosse Pointes. And finally, even the Detroit River had pleasant attributes to offer.

As stated in *Picturesque Detroit and Environs*, an 1893 photo book of Detroit, the river offered

> *the pure bracing qualities of the air and the ever changing interest of the scenes along the River...the vast coming and going, the meeting and greeting of the fleets of the Great Lakes. Huge freighters, modelled and proportioned to equal ocean going craft, mammoth passenger boats bound for Duluth, Milwaukee, Green Bay, Chicago, Cleveland, or Buffalo, great tow barges, grain, lumber and ore carriers, steam yachts, whalebacks, sailing yachts and in fact all kinds of marine travelers, abound in profusion at all points, so that there is no such thing at any point, or any time, as loneliness.*

Experience It

You can get a sense of what the Detroit River shore was like in Cadillac's time by visiting Detroit River Walk. A section of the River Walk has been restored to the original conditions. For a sense of what the Detroit wilderness was like, hike the nature trails on Belle Isle.

You can visit Bloody Run. The creek still flows, although now it runs through Elmwood Cemetery, just east of downtown Detroit.

In the News

Epitome of the Week

A fire in the Scotten tobacco works at Detroit, Mich., caused a loss of $300,000, and two firemen were killed and two others were injured.

—Griggs Courier, *December 12*

Striking Miners

The striking miners (in Ishpeming, MI) held a meeting yesterday, 2,500 miners being present. A committee was appointed to submit a compromise to the company.

—Detroit Free Press, *October 9*

Michigan in Doubt

The alleged Democratic landslide in Michigan is likely to prove no landslide at all; in fact, it is now claimed that the entire Republican state ticket with the exceptions of Turner for Governor and Houston for Attorney General will probably be found to have more votes when the official figures are ferreted out.

—News and Observer, *November 9*

2

1901

Otto stepped up to the bar at J.H. Schooff's saloon at the corner of Clay Street and Jos. Campau Avenue. "It's time to act," he said. "We have to do this to protect our self."

"From what?" came a cynical voice from the small group of men gathered by the bar. "Higher taxes, for sure," said Otto. "If Detroit takes over, you can bet we will pay for it. And what will we get? Nothin', you bet."

"Maybe water lines and sewers and lights," the man responded.

"Yah, maybe," said Otto. "Our money, for sure."

Otto had reason to voice concern. As the nineteenth century turned into the twentieth, Detroit was expanding, pushing its borders ever northward and approaching the small collection of houses and commercial buildings along Jos. Campau Avenue where it was bisected by the rail line. That's where the viaduct is today. Technically, this was still a part of Hamtramck Township but distinct in that it had developed more than the surrounding area. Businesses had begun to locate in the area. We've already mentioned the Russel Iron Works and Acme paint company back in the 1890s, but by now, a mere ten years later, they were joined by the American Radiator Works and Rumsey Manufacturing Company, all clustered near the rail line.

Gradually, new sounds began to be heard. The noises of nature were being fused with the clanging of steel presses, the hiss of boilers, the pounding of heavy machinery. The rumble of moving trains became more prominent. Even slow-moving trains produce an impressive chorus of creaks, grinds and strains generated by the steel wheels rolling along. The air, too, changed, subtly at first, but increasingly, the odors of heavy industry began

Jos. Campau Avenue was a muddy thoroughfare populated by horses and buggies when the twentieth century arrived. This was to soon change greatly with the arrival of immigrants and automobiles.

to spread across the area. It became especially noticeable because the new factories were locating literally next door to houses. That was convenient if you happened to work in one of those factories since you could easily walk to work. On the downside, the smoke-belching, noisy factories were not agreeable neighbors. This situation would grow far worse in the coming years as more and larger factories opened in town.

Industry wasn't the only odor maker shaping the street scene. Schooff's saloon, where Otto voiced his alarm, was just one of an amazing number of saloons that would pack the community. The distinctive smell of mash would become common for decades.

Also growing was the sense of unease among many residents that Hamtramck was going to be swallowed up by the city of Detroit. And why not? After all, it was, at this point, in 1900, just another neighborhood in Hamtramck Township. And so far, Detroit had had no difficulty in annexing portions of Hamtramck, seemingly at will, although there was a process that had to be followed, including a vote and approval of the state, before an annexation could be done. Then there were those rail lines. They were custom-made to serve factories and connected the area to downtown Detroit and distances far beyond in all directions. Much of the area was still undeveloped, meaning there was a lot of room for businesses to grow. Detroit manufacturers were beginning to realize this and looking over the local landscape.

One drawback, however, is that despite the rail lines and the dimensions that Hamtramck would grow to, it never had a train depot. In fact, it was the only town of its size in the nation that didn't have a train depot. However, that didn't deter real estate speculators. They would charter trains and bring prospective land buyers to a makeshift depot on Conant Avenue, just south of Holbrook Creek. There they would be met by a band that would lead them to a picnic ground in Dickinson Woods, an area that is now just south of Veterans Memorial Park, and be served sandwiches and drinks to make them more susceptible to the sales pitch they were going to get.

In 1900, Hamtramck had just a few hundred residents. Most of the community was clustered alongside Jos. Campau Avenue south of the Holbrook ditch. A revealing description of the area appeared in the Hamtramck Public School Bulletin of May 1931. It was titled "The Hamtramck of Yester-Year" by Frank Shultheis, custodian, Junior High School Building. He wrote:

Not many of those who view the thickly populated area of Hamtramck, with its paved streets and sidewalks today, can visualize the great willow swamp which was Hamtramck but a few years ago. There was a country ditch on Holbrook Avenue, twenty feet wide and twelve feet deep, with a bridge crossing it at the intersection with Jos. Campau Avenue. During the spring thaws, when the water was high in this ditch, the fish would come up to spawn. Often I would stand where the Peoples Wayne County Bank is now (southeast corner of Jos. Campau and Holbrook Avenue) and using a pitchfork as a spear, would get enough fish in a short time the supply our table.

There was a high board fence on the west side of Jos. Campau Avenue, running from Holbrook to Caniff. In the winter the snow would blow through this fence and pile on the road in such high drifts that I would have to drive my team through where the alleys are now.

Coming along Holbrook Avenue at that time of year, one was always in great danger of being swept into the deep ditch. The citizens of Hamtramck in those days would walk beside their horses, trying to keep the sleigh from skidding into the water, for fear of sliding with the team and sleigh at some very slippery place. On one or two occasions I have felt very uncomfortable as I tried to get horses, harness, and sleigh untangled, while standing knee-deep in icy water.

The only store in town was on the corner of Jos. Campau and Alice Street. There was a frame building at the corner of Holbrook Avenue at

Jos. Campau that the farmers called "The Coffee Mill." This marked the halfway point to Detroit.

To reach my barn in the spring (my house was right where the Junior High building is now next to the Senior High School between Hewitt and Wyandotte streets west of Jos. Campau Avenue) I would often have to walk out on a makeshift bridge built of boards placed on saw-horses. Where the Senior High School building stands was a corn field. In plowing up this field for the excavation of that building I lost my gold initial ring. So, somewhere underneath the building in which I work is my ring, and I have just about given up hopes of ever finding it.

There is no record of him recovering the ring. It likely is still buried in the ground there.

Schooff's bar was just one of many saloons in town. Despite the relatively small population, there was always enough drinkers to support the local bars. Anthony Buhr had a saloon just down Jos. Campau Avenue not far from Joseph Grix's saloon. Otto visited them all. And with good reason. The bars were rapidly becoming the centers of power in Hamtramck. In 1898, Tony Buer got together with fifteen other local businessmen, fourteen of whom operated saloons, and formed the town's first fraternal charitable organization, the Hamtramck Indians. The club was dedicated "to aid, assist and help their fellow man." They sponsored charitable events to raise money for the needy. And they drank a lot. By 1900, the organization was growing and had fifty members in 1904. Buhr was inspired to base the organization on Indians thanks to a childhood memory of attending traveling shows that featured Indians, or people dressed as Indians, who had performed Wild West–type shows in open lots in the area. Members of the Hamtramck Indians would dress up as Indians for events. They sponsored dances, trips, card parties and raffles into the 1970s, when the group disbanded.

But most Hamtramck residents were neither Indians nor bar owners. They were small farmers who raised crops to be sold to Detroiters. Otto was different in that he worked in one of the factories in town. He lived in a house close to Jos. Campau Avenue with his wife and a young child. She shopped at Thomas Ferguson's grocery store at Alice Street and Jos. Campau Avenue and sometimes at Gottfried Bopps's grocery at the corner of Whiting Street and Jos. Campau. Otto knew his daughter would attend the Holbrook School, which had opened several years earlier on Alice Street, just west of Jos. Campau. There wasn't much to do in the way of entertainment, but on special occasions, when he had enough money saved up, he and the family

Anthony Buhr's saloon on Jos. Campau Avenue was typical for the time. Such saloons were plentiful in the village and served as political gathering spots as well as drinking establishments.

could take a ride on the Baker Street Car to downtown Detroit, which was brimming with shops, theaters, restaurants and more. The Baker line was extended into this area on Jos. Campau to Denton Street. The fare was five cents a person and five cents for each parcel carried up to twenty pounds.

It wasn't a lavish lifestyle, but it was sufficient to get by, and he wanted to preserve it. He promoted his message that Detroit wanted to take over Hamtramck, and it wouldn't be good for the town, which had developed its own sense of community. And people listened. More Hamtramckans began to worry that their town was in danger.

This reached the ears of several prominent residents, including C.A. Fields, H. Mueller, W. Blank, W. Dickinson and J. Hawkins. They called for a community meeting to be held in Holbrook School, where the majority voted for the Village of Hamtramck to be formed. The village connotation is a legal designation. In Michigan, there are three forms of municipalities: cities, townships and villages. There is an unofficial designation of unincorporated towns, which means they are just groups of people living in the same area. That essentially is what Hamtramck in this area was before

The Acme Quality Paint Company (formerly Acme White Lead Paint Company) stood along the railroad lines at the south end of Hamtramck. Neal's Carriage Paint was one of the early products provided by the Acme paint company before the onset of the auto generation.

it incorporated as a village. Villages have certain limitations, such as sharing some services with townships. Villages, like cities and townships, have elected officials, including a president and village council.

Technically, the state government has the final say over all forms of government and can dissolve a city, township or village as it sees fit. But having a village designation makes it harder for a city to annex a nearby municipality. In order for that to happen, the people of the village would have to hold an election and approve the annexation. And the state would have to approve that. This process is complicated and not easy to do. However, it does occur. In the early 2000s, the City of Pontiac, Michigan, annexed a portion of adjoining Bloomfield Township. But it was an awfully messy political battle that created a lot of hard feelings.

It isn't clear how many people were living in the village of Hamtramck at the time it was formed. There are conflicting numbers. Village council minutes of 1901 state the village had a population of 1,454 residents. However, a "Historical Sketch" of Hamtramck prepared by the city as part of the engineer office states there were 500 residents in the village and cites the *Polish Daily Record* as its source. Still another document, the Michigan Historical Records Survey, reprinting the minutes of the village council meetings of 1907–8, notes the village had 300 residents when formed.

Even less clear is how the boundaries of the new roughly 2.1-square-mile village were determined. At a special meeting of the village council held on September 16, 1901, the council approved an expenditure of $1,000 to have a village map drawn up. There are references to village employees taking measuring chains (a common surveying technique) to measure the borders, but it doesn't say how Hamtramck acquired its odd shape. There are some tantalizing clues in early maps of the area that show property lines of farms corresponding with the village borders. But there are individual lots existing today that are partially in Hamtramck and partly in Detroit.

It seems that from the earliest days, Hamtramck would find ways to make simple things difficult. That is a trait that has defined the town to this day. But it's safe to say that was on no one's mind on August 29, 1901, when the first village council met. Their first action was to announce the winners of the first municipal election: Anson Harris was named village president; Henry Jacobs was elected clerk; Henry Krause was assessor; John Heppner was treasurer; and William Hawkins, Ernest Oehmke, Henry Mueller, Joseph Segrist, J. Berres and Martin Wojcinski were named councilmen.

The first council meeting was held in a house owned by Mrs. H. Sawtell at the corner of Denton Street and Jos. Campau. The council approved a payment of $100 to use the building for a year. The council also approved a monthly salary of $9 for the village clerk, $10 for the treasurer, $6 for the janitor and $2.50 for the light tender. This was in the days before the village had electric streetlights, and a tender was needed to light the oil lights along the south end of Jos. Campau Avenue. To save money, the council ordered

that the lights not be lit when the moon was bright.

Jos. Campau was still a dirt road, and along most of its length south of Holbrook Creek, there were wooden sidewalks. Wood frame houses were mixed in with the few commercial buildings that lined the street. It had a strong rural feel. Truck gardens for vegetables to be sold mainly in Detroit were common, and assorted animals roamed freely. In fact, it wasn't until 1916 that the village council passed an ordinance forbidding "geese, ducks, chickens or fowl to run at large anywhere within the limits of the village," and it was the duty of the village marshal to pick up any such loose animals and take them to the village pound.

However, Hamtramck did have a post office on Jos. Campau Avenue. It was known as the Kraft Post Office because it was in the grocery store of Mary Kraft at the corner of Denton Street. In December 1901, the village council passed a resolution renaming it as the Hamtramck Post Office. In 1915, a proper brick post office building would be built at the corner of Jos. Campau Avenue and Dan Street. Robert J. Gallagher served as first postal superintendent, and Gallagher Street was named after him.

In 1940, Emile DeProsse, who had been postal superintendent from 1913 to 1933, recalled that Hamtramck in its early days was "all prairie" north of Caniff Street. "What houses there were were spread out, and industry was grouped along the Michigan Central Railroad," on the south side of town.

You can almost get a sense of empowerment from the village council as they assumed control. The council also flexed its muscles with a local business. The council passed a motion "that the clerk be instructed to notify the Detroit Brewing Company that the conditions of their premises on Arthur Street in Hamtramck Village are in very unhealthy condition and the same constitutes a public nuisance as reported by the Village health officer, and said company to be notified to attend to same at once by order of Village council." The Detroit Brewing Company was a major area brewery that produced 100,000 barrels of beer annually at its brewery

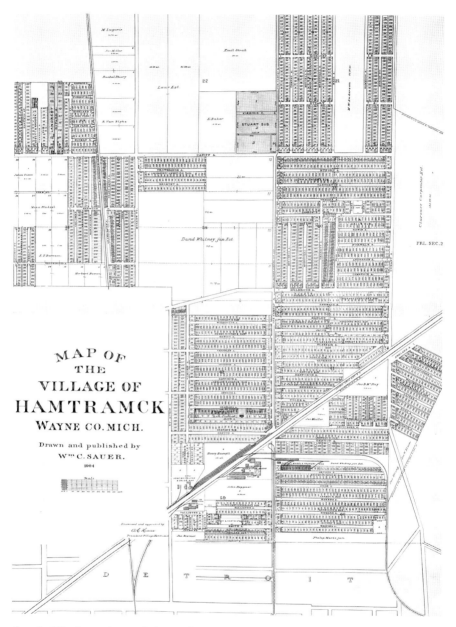

MAP OF
THE
VILLAGE OF
HAMTRAMCK
WAYNE CO. MICH.

Drawn and published by
Wᵐ C. SAUER.
1904

Opposite: Wooden mains carried water in the early days of the village of Hamtramck. The village council focused heavily on putting in water lines from Detroit.

Above: Hamtramck was sparsely populated in 1904 when this village map was created.

at Orleans and Adelaide Streets in downtown Detroit. The council also approved a motion to install a light at the railroad crossing on Jos. Campau.

A much more significant action taken by the council was to approve a motion to contact Detroit to find out how much it would cost to install a water system in town. The estimate came in at $88,000. A special election was held in November 1901, and voters gave the council the go-ahead to issue bonds to cover construction costs. Over the next several years, increasing attention—and money—would be directed to installing sidewalks and sewers. Step by step, Hamtramck was shedding its rural nature and becoming more metropolitan.

An interesting sidelight to the water bond proposal gave a hint of the turbulent times the village was going to face, which has reverberations even today. In order to inform voters about the special election for the bond issue, the council ordered that "dodgers," or fliers, be printed explaining the issue—in German. That reflected that Germans made up a large part of the population of Hamtramck at that time. They were farmers drawn to the area, as it was drained of marshes and turned into productive farmland.

The election ballot of village officers is smattered with German names—George Mertz, Martin Kumm, Henry Krause, Henry Mueller and more. In subsequent years, even more German names appear in the records—Councilmen Zinow, Faber, Buhr and Geimer, and even laborers hired by the council to do jobs like street repairs reflect German heritage—A.R. Schultz, Albert Voss, Henry Derflinger, among many others. Hamtramck was developing as a German community, which is neither good nor bad—unless you were a Polish immigrant with ties to the "Old Country," as was common at the time. The history of Poland and Germany (particularly Prussia) is filled with conflict and animosity on both sides. But it did lead to the dissolution of Poland as a nation in 1795. The area that had been Poland was partitioned three times by Prussia, Austria and Russia. It was a geographical, political and social mess that spurred enormous animosity among all the groups involved, especially the Poles, who suffered through a period of Germanifaction until Poland was restored as a nation in the wake of World War I. The hostility was so sharp that a common nineteenth-century saying was, "As long as the world stands, a Pole and a German will not be brothers."

While the rebirth of Poland was nearly two decades away when Hamtramck village was formed, it was during this period a number of Poles immigrated to the United States specifically to avoid being drafted into the German or Russian armies. Some settled in Hamtramck. But at this time there didn't seem to be much friction between the local Germans and Poles, possibly because there was little competition between the two groups. There was no struggle for political power at this point. And the attention of the civic leaders was on forming a community separate from Detroit and, to their credit, bringing it to the standards of a modern community. The minutes of village council meetings for the next several years after 1901 are filled with proposals to pave streets and install sewers and water lines. The meeting on November 16, 1907, was typical. It contained this resolution proposed by Trustee Zinow and supported by Trustee Kramer:

> *Resolved, That is necessary and expedient to make a public improvement in the village of Hamtramck, Wayne County, Michigan, to be and consist of the construction of a lateral sewer system in the alleys between Andrus and Danforth Avenues from Lumpkin Avenue to the west line or Corliss and Andrus subdivision in said village of Hamtramck, to be known and designated as lateral sewer system No. 17, with the necessary connections to the trunk sewers of said village and this Council hereby determines and orders that said lateral sewer system be constructed.*

Strip off the rhetoric, and this is a plan to put in a sewer line to serve the residents. In the process, the usual ditch alongside the road would be made obsolete, and a potential source of bad odors and disease would be eliminated. This was a time when outhouses were still the norm. Most houses in the village were being constructed on small lots with a barn behind a short backyard. In the barn would be an outhouse. In addition to the smells and unsanitary conditions, using the outhouse during the night in a Michigan winter was challenging and mighty uncomfortable.

Aside from that, life in the village could be fairly monotonous. If you were a farmer, you dealt with the unending task of planting and harvest. Most of Hamtramck's farmers were relatively small scale, raising just enough crops to sell at markets in town and in Detroit and to area businesses. Farmers set their own hours to work, but there was always something to do. Factory work was more rigid, with set days and hours of work. And as the factories grew larger, the strain increased as well. Prior to the widespread use of the assembly line system by Henry Ford, most factory workers built parts and assembled individual items. The assembly line, while far more practical and efficient, added a dimension of monotony to the daily grind. It got worse the larger the factories grew. In summer, the temperature in the factories in the days before air conditioning could rise well above one

Outhouses were common into the early twentieth century. Some remained in use into 1950. They were unsanitary and dangerous.

hundred degrees Fahrenheit. Work could be torturous. Such conditions were exhausting and made workers more prone to have accidents. It was little wonder that the number of saloons increased, both in neighborhoods and near the burgeoning factories. Excessive drinking wasn't noted as a problem in the village at this time, but the Prohibition movement was gaining ground nationally and would figure prominently in Hamtramck in the years ahead. The quality of drinking water was poor at this time, and many people drank beer or other alcoholic beverages—not necessarily to get drunk but because they were safer than well water or worse, stream water.

Alcohol did become important in another way, as the local bars became more than social sites. They became centers of political power, a peculiar situation that was to remain true well into the twentieth century. But in a way, it made sense. Virtually all the men gathered at the saloons, where politics was a frequent topic of discussion. Bartenders developed a huge network of contacts, especially if they were willing to give a guy a free beer now and then. That kind of friendship loyalty could be translated into votes or political influence. Through the years, many Hamtramck politicians had connections to bars and in fact owned bars.

Village Trustee Charles Faber was one of the more prominent bar operators when Jos. Campau was still a dirt road. Like just about everything else at the time, his bar was on the town's South End, an imaginary border defined by Holbrook Creek (later Holbrook Avenue). But the most prominent bar was Munchinger's Saloon and Restaurant on Jos. Campau at the Michigan Central Railroad tracks. Munchinger's evolved into the German political power center of the village but remained part of the network of bars. Proprietor William Munchinger even helped Faber in his push to get a sewer line installed near Faber's bar in 1908.

The prior year had seen a swing in the moral compass of the town when the Archdiocese of Detroit began exploring the idea of establishing a Polish Catholic church in the area. Detroit's Polish community was growing at a rapid rate. Centered originally in the old "Poletown" community area, at Canfield and St. Aubin Streets, about two miles south of Hamtramck, Poles were being attracted north by the increasing number of industries. In 1898, St. Stanislaus Parish was established on Dubois Street south of what would become the village of Hamtramck. It wasn't exceptionally far away, but getting to the church meant a long walk or wagon ride, including over railroad tracks, for Hamtramck parishioners. It seemed logical to establish a new parish directly in the village. That led to the creation of St. Florian Parish.

A vaudeville theater (*at left*) and mud characterized Jos. Campau Avenue in the village days. This is looking north, with Berres Street at the right.

After surveying the community, the archdiocese determined that there was support for a new Polish parish despite Hamtramck's largely German, Lutheran population. Initial masses were held in Matt Berres's shoe store on Jos. Campau. Soon two residents donated the land where the church now stands to the archdiocese for the construction of a combination church and school. In 1909, it was constructed.

This should not be underestimated. St. Florian would play a critical role in the formation and growth of modern Hamtramck. It was far more than a community parish, as its influence grew greatly. That wasn't expected or obvious in its early years. But it and its industrial counterpart, the Dodge Main factory, were essential to the very existence of Hamtramck today.

Hamtramck was now poised for great changes. The foundation was in place as the village developed after 1901. Empty lots were being filled, and farmland was being platted into neighborhoods with lots designated for housing. The quiet, dark nights that defined the area just a handful of years earlier were being rattled by the clacking of trains passing through and the rhythmic metal beat of the streetcars moving across the south end of town. Soon they would be making their way all through the village. Years later, a grandmother would recall her earliest memory as a child held in her mother's arms, being lulled to sleep by the sounds of the passing streetcars. Cows were making their last stand in the open fields that were disappearing into the hands of developers. It was becoming clear that Hamtramck was on the road to a much more dynamic and dramatic future.

And as for Otto, who gave the dire warning that Hamtramck was facing oblivion if it didn't become a village, he got a job at the Dodge Main factory and worked there for thirty years before retiring as a lifelong resident of Hamtramck.

Experience It

For a direct contact with this period of time, go to Holbrook Elementary School between Alice and Grayling Streets. It was here that a group of residents gathered in 1900 and agreed to establish the Village of Hamtramck.

In the News

Probably Murdered

Paul Reno, a farmer living alone on Jefferson Ave., in Grosse Pointe Township, near the city limits was burned to death early today. All circumstances surrounding his death point to a conviction that he was murdered, and his house set on fire to conceal the crime.

—St. Paul Globe, *March 26*

Detroit Suppresses Langtry

Mayor Mayberry of Detroit, who witnessed "The Degenerates" at Toledo the other night, threatened to revoke the opera house franchise in Detroit if the play was put on there, and so it was given to Windsor, Ont., a little Canadian town across the river from Detroit.

—Weekly Independent, *April 13*

Cockran at Detroit

For two hours and a quarter tonight Bourke Cockran, of New York, discussed "imperialism" before an enthusiastic audience of 5,000 persons at Light Guard Armory.

—News and Observer, *October 18*

3

1910

John and Horace Dodge stepped up to the challenge of facing down Henry Ford. It wasn't a case of animosity. They were all businessmen and respected each other. Ford, in fact, admired the quality of the work the Dodges did. They were engineers who had their own machine shop in downtown Detroit where they manufactured parts for Ford beginning in February 1903. Ford was on his third attempt to start a car company and was headed for success. But no one knew that then, and Ford was still cash-strapped. He owed the Dodges money for parts he had ordered from them, and in lieu of money, he gave them 10 percent of the stock of the Ford Company. But their partnership wasn't destined to last. Ford manufactured cars, and sales took off like rockets. In 1904, Ford moved his operations from a rented building on Mack Avenue in Detroit to a larger facility at Piquette Street, a short distance farther north. That allowed for greater production and increased sales. It also increased the demand for Dodge-made parts. With each year, both the Dodge brothers and Ford felt the growing pressure for more space.

Ford turned his attention farther north to the village of Highland Park, which slightly abutted the village of Hamtramck. He selected a good location, right on Woodward Avenue and adjoining a rail line. The streetcar line also ran down Woodward and could deliver employees right to the plant. As Ford was exploring opening a new, bigger factory, the Dodges were facing the same dilemma: business was better than they could handle, at least at their plant on Monroe Street in downtown Detroit. They,

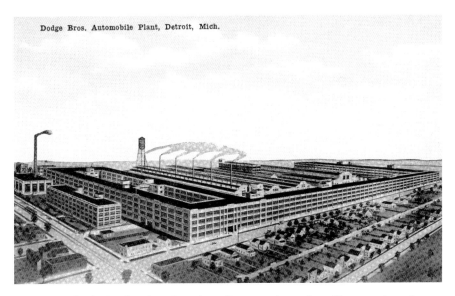

Dodge Bros. Automobile Plant, Detroit, Mich.

In 1909, the Dodge brothers bought a piece of property in southern Hamtramck, and within a few months, the first manufacturing buildings were up. Their factory would become known as Dodge Main and grow to a massive size.

too, looked north, but settled on Hamtramck village as the place for the new factory they were envisioning.

The Dodges found dusty, dirty Hamtramck attractive for a number of reasons. It was well located. The village was about five miles from the Detroit River, and there were some substantial roads, like Chene Street, Dequindre Street and Conant Avenue, connecting it to the downtown area. Even more significant, the site in Hamtramck they were looking at was only a mile or so away from the new factory that Henry Ford was building in the village of Highland Park. And rail lines from the south and west sides of Hamtramck led directly to the Ford site, so shipping parts from here to there would be easy. And Hamtramck was an independent village, with a tax rate about half that of the city of Detroit. Finally, the Dodges were not naïve. They knew that Ford was moving toward becoming self-sufficient, and eventually he would cut out most suppliers, including the Dodge brothers.

Finally, the Dodges wanted to manufacture their own cars. They had the skills and reputation to do it. So their vision of the future was clear, and that wide-open space at the south end of the village of Hamtramck was just what they wanted. The brothers wasted no time in buying the property in September 1909 and hiring noted architect Albert Kahn to design the initial sections of the factory complex, including a forge, blacksmith shop, machine shop and offices. By early 1910, buildings were being constructed for the new factory. They were still building parts for Fords but were getting ready to launch their own cars.

Hamtramck was also on the launching pad to the future. Although it was still largely rural, that was swiftly changing. Holbrook Creek was gone,

By the second decade of the twentieth century, Hamtramck was acquiring a national reputation as an industrial town.

neighborhoods were being platted and housing construction had begun in earnest. On July 2, 1910, the *Detroit Times* carried a story under the heading "Real Estate Booming in Hamtramck Village." It listed an impressive roster of lots and houses that had been recently sold: "House and lot on south side of Edwin-ave., the village of Hamtramck, between Jos. Campau and Whitney-aves. [later named Brombach Street], lot 30-x100 feet, for the Whitney Realty Company, Ltd., to Joseph Traczynski, for $1,600," was typical. And more were being listed as the neighborhoods began to take shape.

The news that the Dodge brothers were moving to town contributed to the coming building boom. Soon lots, mainly on the south side of the village, were being platted for houses. Most of the lots were small, thirty by one hundred feet, as the newspaper article mentioned. There was (and is) barely five feet of space between houses. And most of the houses being built were multifamily units, some housing four families on two floors. Given that families tended to be large in those days, partially because so many children died in infancy, the new neighborhoods were instantly crowded. Builders were clamoring for the opportunity to help with the development of the village. "Planned to Make Great City of Hamtramck" was the awkwardly worded headline in the *Detroit Times* edition of February 10, 1910. The story focused on the attempt of two men, Arthur C. O'Connor and Matthew Finn, to obtain franchises to expand public utilities in the village, especially transportation. O'Connor was an attorney who had worked with industrial companies to help locate them in Hamtramck. Finn was a Detroit bond dealer who no doubt would handle the financial side of the operations if the village council embraced their plans to open the town to more industry. At first, the council was not convinced these two men could bring about such a major industrialization of the village. But their efforts did make it clear that Hamtramck was on a new course of development and quickly leaving its rural past behind.

So who was backing them? No one knew, and there was speculation that a consortium of factory owners wanted the village to incorporate as a city, annex the remaining portions of Hamtramck Township and build some sort of industrial empire. It was not as far-fetched as it may have seemed. Industries saw Hamtramck as a business haven. Already the Acme White Lead Paint Company, Russel Wheel and Foundry and Swedish Crucible plants were operating in the town, the Dodges were setting up shop there and more companies were eyeing the village. Soon the roster of industries would include many more.

"The southern and western portions of Hamtramck are now virtually portions of Detroit, industrially, the territory being about as well built up on

Houses and factories huddled together on crowded streets without the slightest concern about proper zoning. Examples of that are still seen today.

one side of the boundary as on the other," the *Detroit Times* noted. "It is a matter of only a few years until this portion of the village will be as solidly built up as most of the city."

However, a big roadblock to locating and expanding in the village was a lack of transportation. The Detroit Urban Railroad ran a line into town, but it ended at Denton Street and it was far too small to handle the growing demand of the increasing workforce living in the area.

"There are few improvements in Hamtramck at the present time," the article continued. "With a sure prospect of a big population, the village has mud streets and is but partially lighted and sewered as yet. It must get a great many improvements all at once as soon as the factories now building or projected, are completed, and the workingmen employed therein move into the locality."

"Hamtramck has a tax rate half that of Detroit and will have a low tax rate for years. It is the ideal spot for factories. But there must be street cars to carry the people and other improvements must be provided. That is vital," O'Connor told the village council. The *Detroit Times* article was just one of a stream of newspaper and magazine stories about the remarkable transformation going on in Hamtramck. Hamtramck wasn't the only town to industrialize. After all, Detroit was once an expanse of swamps and forests. But few places in the nation were undergoing such a rapid and radical change as Hamtramck.

O'Connor and Finn won over the council, and they agreed to put the measure on the ballot. The street rail franchise was approved by a vote of 229 to 128 and the electric franchise by a vote of 228 to 126. This opened the way for streetcar lines to progress, which would be critical to provide transportation for the workers at the growing number of factories. Changes were coming, and the development was cementing Hamtramck's reputation as an industrial center. The village was featured on the cover of *Michigan Manufacturer* magazine on December 2, 1911, with an article titled "Hamtramck—Detroit's Most Remarkable Suburb."

As manufacturers took notice of the town, so did potential employees. Just south of Hamtramck in Detroit stretched the massive Poletown neighborhood. Roughly, it spanned the area between Hamtramck's southern border, Gratiot Avenue, Woodward Avenue and Van Dyke Avenue. It developed with the first Polish immigrant influx in the mid-nineteenth century. At the core of Poletown

was St. Albertus Church at the intersection of St. Aubin and Canfield Streets. Its troubled early years and a parishioner conflict with the founding of the neighboring Sweetest Heart of Mary Parish brought the neighborhood wider attention. Newspapers covering the turmoil, which resulted in the death of a man, started referring to the neighborhood as Poletown because the majority of residents were Polish immigrants. The tangled, contentious story of Poletown is too complicated to relate here, but the neighborhood had an abundant supply of workers who were quickly drawn to Hamtramck and its growing number of factories.

The draw wasn't limited to Detroit. Workers from as far away as Pennsylvania and New York traveled to the metro Detroit area for jobs. Many found their way to Hamtramck. Some were single men who rented space in rooming houses. Conditions were sparse. A typical room

Single men often immigrated to Hamtramck for jobs at the factories. Many rented rooms, barely eight feet by ten feet in area. It was just enough space for a bed and small corner sink. Toilets were down the hall.

might be no more than eight by ten feet, with a small sink in the corner and a miniscule closet, barely three feet long. But that was enough considering that the average working man might have three sets of clothes: a work outfit, an everyday shirt and pants and a suit for going to church on Sunday. Married couples might rent a three-room apartment consisting of a kitchen, living room and bedroom. Another arrangement would be an upper flat. This might have two bedrooms, a kitchen and a living room. And those who successfully settled here would buy a house, possibly a bungalow or simple two-story frame structure. In most cases, none of these had indoor bathrooms at first—although the village officials made an effort to end the use of outhouses as soon as sewer lines were made available.

Sometimes the immigrants might rent a flat in a home owned by a Black family, so there were cases when Black and White families lived in the same house, something that was virtually unheard of anywhere else in the country. This was indicative of the complex story of Black and White relations that will be explored later.

Regardless of the accommodations, the one feature all the sites shared was closeness. The fast-developing neighborhoods were rapidly filling up with residents, putting an ever-increasing strain on the village government. Demands for services were growing, and the village council was hard-pressed to respond. In this period, virtually every village council meeting was dominated by a proposal to expand sewer and water lines along some street, or there were complaints about the unpaved muddy streets and the need for real sidewalks, made of concrete, not wooden planks.

The kids didn't seem to mind, and they were everywhere. However, there were no playgrounds in the village, so most kids played ball in empty lots, some along Jos. Campau Avenue, and on the streets. Jos. Campau Avenue was still largely undeveloped. Most businesses were clustered on the south side of town along Jos. Campau Avenue mixed in with houses. Anufry Sawicki had his grocery store conveniently next to Julius Zielinski's bakery at Smith Street, just south of the railroad tracks. A block north, Edward Russell operated a saloon across the street from the Cooper Brothers saloon. A block north of the railroad tracks was Munchinger's popular bar. Then came Frederick Fisher's shoe store where Leuschner (Miller) Street met Jos. Campau Avenue and the S. Ploter dry good store. H.C. Vollmar's confectionery was at the corner of Berres Street while Peter Konen, George Forbes and Frederick Rooks lived along Jos. Campau Avenue between Danforth and Goodson Streets. And so it went until Evaline Street, where the line of businesses and homes abruptly stopped. From here on there were farms and open spaces.

Little thought was given to recreation in early Hamtramck. Kids played in empty lots and on the muddy streets.

Auto traffic was rare until after the Dodge plant was built in 1910, and then it became a serious problem that lingered for years. It became increasingly common for kids—and adults—to be hit by cars, which eventually led the police department to develop a traffic bureau. The police department, which consisted of one officer on a bicycle in 1901, grew to a handful of officers in 1915 before greatly expanding by the early 1920s. But this would prove to be painfully inadequately, especially when Prohibition went into effect.

However, as talk of Prohibition grew, so did the number of bars in town. Jos. Campau Avenue, where most were located, began to develop, reaching farther northward. Additionally, more corner stores opened. These would appear on almost every street. Small, usually dingy and with limited items for sale, they would provide for the day-to-day needs of the nearby residents. Almost no one had cars, so folks had to walk to do their shopping, and there were no refrigerators in homes, just iceboxes. These were better than nothing, but not much. Iceboxes were literally that—upright wooden boxes that were cooled by blocks of ice. Usually, they consisted of a set of shelves and a space to place the block of ice. As the ice melted, the water dripped into a container at the bottom of the icebox. Ice had to be replenished often, and each day a wagon pulled by a horse would come down the street. The homeowner, usually the woman who did the cooking, would signal out a window or from the porch with her outstretched hand or hands if she wanted a five- or ten-pound block, which would be brought to her door. Some folks were a little fancier and had the icebox on a porch with an opening in back that connected to a small door in a wall that opened to the outside. The iceman could then deliver the ice through the door directly into the icebox. Seems mighty inconvenient and inefficient, but it worked, at least somewhat.

Many homes had root cellars where vegetables and other foods could be kept cool in the summer and warm enough not to freeze in the winter. People also grew vegetables in their backyards for canning. In many ways, life in the 1910s was a curious blend of rural and urban. For some, it was an improvement on their lives; for others it was an evolutionary change that they adapted to, and for the immigrants it was a cultural shock that could be nightmarish. Yet the factories brought jobs, which were hailed by the growing population as an improvement in the community. But the change in the physical and social landscape came at a big cost, especially as more Polish immigrants came to the village. Some immigrants moved only a short distance from Detroit to Hamtramck. Others were fairly new to America, having lived in New York, Pennsylvania or other eastern areas before journeying to Hamtramck. Still others came here almost directly from Poland where almost all had lived on farms. So in a short period,

With industry came pollution. Smokestacks began to compete with trees in defining the horizon. At least eleven smokestacks can be seen in this photo taken from the roof of Holbrook school.

they went from a green landscape where the sounds of cows and sheep roamed to a congested urban jungle where trains roared, factory presses pounded and the air had a peculiar acrid smell that burned their throats. There were no lush mountains in the distance, only the brick and steel walls of a factory built next door to their homes. Wires started to crisscross the sky, and tall trees were subdued under the skyward stretch of a forest of smokestacks. The once bucolic sounds of the countryside were fading fast, and as houses were being built at a furious rate, the pounding hammers and saws would have echoed as the community took shape. It was disruptive, but it was a byproduct of a community in the making.

Many immigrants did not speak English, but they had their neighbors to turn to for support. Also, organizations like the Tau Beta Community House and St. Anne's Community House began offering social services for adults and children. Tau Beta especially developed a strong connection to the immigrant community. Tau Beta has a remarkable history. Established in 1901 by four girls, aged fifteen to sixteen years old, it began as a fairly mindless kids' social club: "A club with a pin to wear all the time, with a constitution and bylaws, and a motto and a grip and a whistle. And we must have an aim—a really good one live up to," they recounted in the official history in 1938. Initially, they spent most of their time planning parties. Deciding that wasn't a sufficient reason for being, they began doing charitable work in the community. They prepared meals and delivered them to the needy across Detroit in conjunction with the Visiting Nurse Association. For these upper-class young girls, it became a life experience.

"We had encountered, and could never ignore afterwards, the unforgettable smell of poverty," Tau Beta historian Mildred Plum wrote.

As the Tau Beta group matured, so did their organization. In November 1916, they rented a flat on Hanley Street for twenty-two dollars a month with the aim of providing social services to the immigrant community. It was a challenging proposition. Their history recounted:

> *Cheaply constructed houses and duplexes were springing up on dozens of unpaved streets. There were, for a long time after we entered the community, large numbers of vacant lots, but there were no playgrounds. The school system was undeveloped, the village government had little vision of the public's needs, and naturally was in no hurry to supply what it did not recognize as essential. We aimed to undertake what the authorities did not, or could not, provide and demonstrate its value until the village council should assume any such burden, relieving us to supply other facilities, until we could eventually wish those, too, unto the council, the schools, or whoever should by rights carry their responsibility.*

At first the local population was leery of these strangers, but they began to respond to the number of social programs being offered there, including cooking and sewing classes, music lessons, gardening programs and much more. Tau Beta also helped people with job referrals, calls for doctors and medical treatments, and the members supplied legal advice and clothes and food for the needy. Their building became known as "the house with the light," for the distinctive, and welcoming, porch light that always burned. In a few years, the flat was replaced by a small building farther west on Hanley Street, and in 1928, a large community center, complete with housing for staff, was built across the street. Tau Beta had an enormous effect on Hamtramck and the local population. Many kids were sent to Tau Beta summer camp to get them away from the heavily polluted industrial air of the city. And Tau Beta established the Hamtramck Public Library. Tau Beta remained operating in Hamtramck until the late 1950s, when the organization decided its services were no longer needed. Its large community house was eventually acquired by the Hamtramck Public Schools and turned into Tau Beta School.

Tau Beta was a product of necessity. So was St. Anne's Community House, which offered similar services but on a smaller scale. Not everyone in Hamtramck was poverty-stricken, but as a whole the village was out of balance. There was an increasing need for services and resources, but as Tau Beta perceptively stated it, the village governing body was incapable of delivering much of anything. Further, the community was beginning to strain under the political pressure of a divided population. In 1901, Germans outnumbered Poles by a margin of about ten to one. But in the later 1910s, that statistic flipped, yet it was still the Germans who maintained control of the powerbase in the village. They were determined to keep it. Initially, the Poles did not focus on politics, but as the population matured and grew to understand the American political system, they started to press their presence on those in power. They demanded that the village hire a person in the clerk's office who could speak Polish. The demand was ignored. Then came reports of voter suppression, of the village closing voting polls on election day before 5:00 p.m. when the factory employees got off from work so they couldn't make it to the polls in time to vote. Finally, rumors were circulating that the German Hamtramck officials were working with Detroit officials to have Hamtramck annexed by Detroit in an arrangement that would leave the local politicians still in power over the area. No evidence has been found that was true, but then, as now, truth is dispensable in the world of politics.

The Poles responded by forming a political movement with the aim of converting Hamtramck into a city. Such a move would make annexation by Detroit virtually impossible. To bolster their ballot power, the Poles turned to the local Black community. Overall, relations between the Black residents and Polish newcomers had been surprisingly cordial. Both groups got along fairly well. It's possible the Poles, who had suffered suppression under the Russians, Prussians (Germans) and Austrians during the nineteenth and early twentieth centuries, felt a sense of understanding for what the Black population had endured in America as slaves and later with the oppression of discrimination. In any case, the coalition was successful, and city status would become a reality.

But leading up to that fateful vote, the village was becoming a hotbed of activity. That was greatly enhanced on May 1, 1917, when Michigan enacted Prohibition. That was nearly three years ahead of the national Prohibition law. Prohibition's effect on Hamtramck was both dramatic and meaningless. Almost overnight, the village was transformed into a town of rebellious lawbreakers. Banks were not being robbed any more than usual, and murders had not suddenly become common. But denying the mainly Polish population the right to buy beer, or any other alcoholic beverage, was viewed as outrageous, and if having a drink meant breaking the law, then so be it. Hamtramck wasn't unique in its feelings toward Prohibition, of course, as nearly the whole nation opposed it, but a drink was one of the few outlets people had at that time to escape the hardships of everyday life, if just for a little while. Alcohol was ingrained in society and tradition. After all, the most

Pool halls were dark and cramped, but they provided a rare place to have some legal fun even during Prohibition.

sacred part of the Christian Mass is to sip wine, representing the blood of Jesus. While the use of alcohol was still allowed for religious purposes, there would be no more drinking at the corner bar.

Or would there be?

Quickly, illegal stills were being installed in houses and commercial buildings across the village. Seemingly everyone was in the business of making booze, either for personal use or to sell. Basements, attics, garages, sheds, factory buildings, any space that could be converted into a brewery or distillery was becoming just that. It didn't take long for the criminal element to get organized and extend their reach throughout the community. Thousands of speakeasies opened in Detroit and Hamtramck. As it turned out, Hamtramck was in an ideal spot. By this time, Detroit had annexed almost all the land around Hamtramck and neighboring Highland Park, and Detroit was fast becoming the main conduit for liquor smuggled in from Canada. A lot of that liquor made its way to Hamtramck, which was popular with Detroiters who wanted to have a drink away from whoever may be watching in Detroit. In 1920, when the rest of the nation joined Michigan in instituting Prohibition, things only got worse.

So as the decade of the teens came to a close, things were boiling in Hamtramck in many ways. The population hit forty-eight thousand, which was far too much for a town of 2.1 square miles and with no high-rise buildings. The village government seemed at a loss to handle the enormous influx of immigrants, mainly Poles, who were organized and determined to take political control of the town. Development was taking place everywhere as the empty lots were fast being filled with new houses. They weren't much, hardly more than giant wooden crates, but as fast as they were built, they were occupied. And while jobs were plentiful, life was still hard.

Walter and Anna experienced it firsthand. They lived in a three-room flat on Alice Street, on the south side of town. They had moved in a year earlier with their two-year-old daughter, Theresa. Walter and Anna were born in Poland, where they grew up on farms, but they didn't meet until their families emigrated from Poland and became neighbors in Pennsylvania. But as soon as they met, they knew they were a match. Walter worked in a mine, which scared Anna terribly. At her urging, he looked for another job, but the only thing he could find was underground.

In the second decade of the twentieth century, the Prohibition movement was gaining momentum. Michigan went dry in 1917. Soon speakeasies and liquor-producing sites were being regularly raided, but that did nothing to stem the flow of liquor.

Then he heard that jobs were plentiful in Detroit. The new auto industry was building factories, and they needed workers. Plus, plenty of other factories were being built by companies that supplied the big auto plants. So he, Anna and young Theresa made their way to Detroit. It was painful to leave their families behind, but they took some comfort in the thought that eventually they would all reunite in Detroit.

Walter didn't find a job in one of the big factories, but he did in a small machine shop that was located just down Lumpkin Street, an easy walking distance from their flat. That was good, because he was paid only nineteen cents an hour and couldn't afford streetcar fare. Plus there was rent, food, clothes and the other basic necessities that cost money. Anna took in laundry, which added to their meager income, but hauling clothes up to the flat, boiling water for washing and using the stove to heat the iron were exhausting. And then there was Theresa, who needed a lot of attention, as little children do. Yet somehow they managed. They were relatively healthy, despite the ever-present risk of exposure to cholera, influenza, smallpox, polio and a host of other diseases that periodically afflicted the community.

On a Sunday afternoon, the only time of the week they were able to find comfort in relaxing, they sat at the kitchen table quietly talking. Theresa was napping, and fortunately their neighbors in the adjoining flat and downstairs were generally quiet. They may have been just too tired to make much noise. Walter and Anna kept their voices low so as not to disturb Theresa. Few outside noises penetrated the house. Occasionally, especially at night, they could hear the passing of a train. There were tracks just a few blocks south and west of them. And there was the ever-present hiss of steam escaping from one factory or another in the neighborhood.

"Maybe Mamma can come for a visit in the fall," Anna said.

Walter nodded, but reluctantly said, "Where will we put her? There isn't enough room for us already."

Anna smiled slightly. "You can sleep in the living room for a while, and she can share the bed with me."

Walter sighed. "Yes," was all he said. He knew how much Anna missed her family and would not deny her a chance to see her mother. But he had made it clear they couldn't afford to pay her train fare. And she would have to help with the cost of food. Anna had sighed, too, but only because she knew her mother would buy food for all of them and provide money for much more. That was another reason Walter didn't object to having her mother visit. As the summer afternoon drifted toward evening, they had a modest supper, but because it was Sunday, they treated themselves

Heavy industry encroached on rural land, creating a stark contrast as Hamtramck made its transition to an industrial town. Reminders of that change can still be found at the south end of the city.

to kielbasa and kapusta. Then they moved to the front porch that looked down over the block. Theresa was awake and active, and they kept a close watch on her so she wouldn't climb the wooden railing. It was a hefty drop to the street below. There was no real sidewalk yet and the street wasn't paved, but the block was filled with houses. Alice Street was one of the oldest in the village, and what had been a farm was transformed into an urban street. Yet there were still tall elm trees lining the street, forming a huge canopy of leaves like the ceiling of a cathedral.

"I think Jozef is making beer," Walter said, having run out of other things to talk about. Jozef lived next door. "In the barn. I see him going in almost every day when I am going to work. And I can smell the mash."

"Well, you keep your nose out of there," Anna said. Prohibition had just become law in Michigan, and the smell of stills cooking was becoming more common. Unable to buy drinks, people began making their own. Soon they would see neighborhood children toting buckets of beer down the block, making deliveries to a growing list of regular customers of brewers who operated stills set up in bathtubs in bathrooms, attics, basements and barns.

Although this was illegal, the police weren't a problem. A few free beers were all it took to make them look the other way.

"My nose is clean," Walter laughed. "But what about your mother?" She liked beer. Anna moaned, "Oh, just be quiet." They slept well that night, and by 6:00 a.m. Walter was up and out, heading to the machine shop. He wouldn't be back until after 6:00 p.m. It was a long, hard day in a sweaty, dirty, noisy factory. Yet it could have been worse. He wasn't going hungry, and Anna and Theresa were well. The rest of the days of the week were much the same. Eventually, he would get a better job in one of the auto plants, where the pay was forty-five cents an hour, and when power of the auto unions strengthened, so did his paycheck. Theresa would go to Holbrook School, just down the street from their flat. Over the years, the family would add a couple more children, and by the time Theresa graduated from Hamtramck High School, the family had bought a house in Hamtramck with a coal furnace, indoor bathroom and plenty of hot water. There Anna and Walter lived out the rest of their lives. The kids all married and moved to the suburbs.

But they kept Hamtramck in their hearts.

Experience It

Clay Street, where it curves to St. Aubin Street at the far southwest corner of Hamtramck, still supports a trace of heavy industry, railroad tracks and trees blended in a mixture that reflects the elements of Hamtramck as it evolved from forests to factories. And take a walk down Alice Street.

In the News

POLISH LABORERS SHOW GREAT ZEAL IN BUILDING UP NEW RESIDENCE DISTRICT IN HAMTRAMCK

Out Hamtramck way, in the north-eastern outskirts of the city, building operations are under way that would astound the average Detroiter whose recollections of this particular section is probably associated with cow pastures.

—Detroit Times, *April 16*

HAMTRAMCK FARMER BLOWS FAVORITE CHILD'S HEAD OFF WITH GUN FOLLOWING QUARREL

"I blame my sons, Sam and George, for all this trouble," said Mark Howcroft, Sr., in talking to a Times reporter in Wayne County jail Monday morning about his killing Mark Howcroft, his youngest son, 23 years old, with a shotgun shortly before 10 o'clock Sunday night.

—Detroit Times, *August 22*

WAYNE COUNTY'S VALUATION JUMP INCREASE IN YEAR IS $21,633,168, DETROIT AND HAMTRAMCK BEING CHIEF CONTRIBUTORS TO BOOST

The growth of Detroit and the whole Wayne County, during the past year, is reflected in a report on the assessment of the city and townships presented during the Monday morning meeting of the board of supervisors. The total assessed valuation is $431,450,901, an increase of 421,633,163 over that of 1909.

—Detroit Times, *October 18*

4

1922

Noisy, smelly, crowded and dirty. And no one was taking any steps to make things better. In fact, that could be viewed as a sign of progress. Hamtramck was booming. Factories were opening within the city boundaries faster than a Dodge car could speed down Jos. Campau. Speaking of which, Hamtramck's most important street was now a city unto itself, a jumbled mix of factories, houses, stores and other buildings. Just to the north of the Dodge Main factory were the Michigan Smelting and Refining Company, the Detroit Bevel Gear Factory, the American Radiator Company and the Russel Wheel & Foundry. Across the street was the Mistele Coal Company. Its coal yard stood alongside the railroad tracks, and later, when the viaduct was built in 1927, train cars bearing coal would perch above bins and drop their loads off the side. The railroad tracks marked the line defining the character of the street. Here houses and stores replaced the factories. Charles Koop operated his barbershop, located just north of the railroad tracks. Two buildings father north was the Van Eeckhoutte & Sons auto part shop. There was a story in that alone. Just a few years earlier, it was Van Eeckhoutte's saloon. But that changed with Prohibition. Such a drastic change was unusual. More typically, the saloons put out of businesses by Prohibition either closed or converted to selling soft drinks. Of course, many of them simply changed their name from "Saloon" to "Confectionary" and continued to sell booze. Village Councilman Charles Faber's saloon, which was next to Van Eeckhoutte, underwent a clean conversion as it became the Andrews & Poppas Restaurant by 1920. That, in turn, was next to Welling's

Railroad tracks, a horse-drawn wagon and an auto parts manufacturing plant encapsulate the industrial history of Hamtramck in one scene.

soft drink parlor at the corner of Denton Street and E. Dowser's soft drink parlor and August Milke's soft drink parlor. Apparently, Hamtramckans had developed an insatiable desire for soda pop. Or maybe…

Moving north was the office of Oram Sugarman, steamship agents. Many Hamtramckans had immediate relatives in Poland at this time, and they were routinely shipping items—and people—across the Atlantic. Isaac Kreman ran a shoe store near Miller Street, and the Hamtramck Laundry was located next to Mrs. C. Knechtel, dressmaker, who was next to T. Schultz & Company, tailors. Across the street was the home of Edward Burlow. Small grocery stores and meat markets also clustered in the area as we approach the old Village Hall, which was built in 1915 between Alice and Grayling Streets. Across the street from Village Hall were the offices of Drs. C.J. Martin, John Graff and Zerxes Jones.

At the corner of Grayling Street was the W.S. Jolliff Auto Livery (sales room). Across the street was Charles Timm's hardware store, and a few doors down was the Union Cooperative bakery. At the corner of Jos. Campau and

Grayling Street stood the Hamtramck Township offices, which were distinct from the village offices. And all along the strip there were more bakeries, hardware stores, shoe stores, barbershops, clothing stores, doctors' offices— everything that one would want and expect to have in a thriving community. Most of the businesses were family operations. At the intersection of Holbrook and Jos. Campau, which only a few years before was the banks of a large creek and the site of the distinctive Dolland farmhouse, now stood the First State Bank of Hamtramck and Hamtramck State Bank. There would be many banks in Hamtramck; few survived the Great Depression. But in the early 1920s, Hamtramck was booming. In many ways it was an ideal situation for the immigrant community. Everything was close. You could walk to work or to the store just down the street. Transportation was limited, but most people didn't have far to go. Families, which formed mutual support systems, could cluster in neighborhoods. Although not much thought was put into the planning of the town, as was evidenced by the jumble of houses, businesses and everything else that constituted the community, it all seemed to work. It was crowded, it could be noisy and the air often was tainted by suspicious industrial odors, but it also had a vibrant sense of community. It was a lively town that had so much to offer, even too much at times, as shown by the "soft drinks" parlors.

And houses were being built everywhere. Seemingly every inch of space was being developed. Parks? A waste of space! The kids can play in empty lots and streets. Property sales were so hot that even the huge J.L. Hudson store in downtown Detroit got into the business of selling property in Hamtramck and had a Hudson's subdivision on the northeast side of town. Stores were opening rapidly all over town, especially along Jos. Campau Avenue north of Holbrook Avenue. In the late 1910s, Jos. Campau was widened north of Caniff Street all the way to the city's northern border at Carpenter Creek, which also ended up drained and replaced by a road. In 1915, Hamtramck High School was built on former farmland between Geimer and Hewitt Streets. And the school population was growing rapidly. It was clear that more schools would have to be built—and soon.

The village was also undergoing a titanic political shift as the Poles pushed their movement to have the Village of Hamtramck incorporate as a city to prevent being annexed by Detroit. In October 1921, the villagers approved the incorporation measure. A city council was elected in early 1922, and the first city charter was written and went into effect on April 3, 1922. Hamtramck was officially born.

With the growth of industry also came an influx of people. Suddenly, land in Hamtramck became exceptionally valuable for housing and factories. Even the J.L. Hudson Company, known for its Downtown Detroit department store, got into the business of selling property in Hamtramck.

The last vestiges of rural Hamtramck were virtually gone. Hamtramck was now an industrial city—for better and for worse. Streetlights were in place, sewer and water lines were being installed and horses pulling wagons had almost completely disappeared (except for some trash collectors, who would roam the city's alleys in horse-pulled carts into the 1960s). But the streetcar line had been extended through the new city, and more autos were appearing on the streets.

But more than anything, there were people. The crowded conditions of the city became intense. Multifamily homes standing just feet apart were the defining character of the neighborhoods. St. Florian Parish was a perfect example of the almost uncontrolled growth that was occurring. The original church-school building at Brombach and Florian Streets became too small almost as soon as it opened. The "basement" church was constructed nearly next to the original school-church building, but it was designed to hold only two thousand people and did almost nothing to relieve the pressure. The congregation grew so large that the parish was split in 1917 to form Our Lady Queen of Apostles Parish on Conant Avenue and split again in 1920 to form St. Ladislaus Parish on Caniff Avenue. By 1922, the St. Florian school

By 1922, cars were becoming common on Jos. Campau Avenue. The street was turning into a major shopping district.

building housed over two thousand students. That was a staggering number for a single elementary school, especially one with such limited physical space. The number of weddings, baptisms and funerals rose accordingly as St. Florian became the second-largest parish in the Archdiocese of Detroit. During the Great Depression, which began in 1929, St. Florian played a critical role in providing aid to families that had been devastated by the economic collapse. The year 1922 also saw the founding of Holy Cross Polish National Catholic Church. In fact, there was a significant number of churches operating in Hamtramck by 1922, including Immaculate Conception Ukrainian Catholic Church, St. Peter's African Methodist Episcopal Church, Corinthian Baptist Church, First Baptist Institutional Church, Macedonia National Baptist Church and Martini Lutheran Church. There were more, but some closed and/or moved to Detroit.

The town certainly had a lot of spirit—and spirits of the most unholy kind, as the full effects of Prohibition settled into place. Politicians and police officers formed alliances with bootleggers. For a small cut of the abundant profits, the bootleggers were given virtually a free hand to brew and distill whatever they wanted. This was separate from the low-level bathtub brewers who made just enough hooch for themselves and their neighbors. The big bootleggers were the folks who operated in factory buildings and breweries that had supposedly switched to making nonalcoholic drinks. Their production was large in scale, but it seemed that no matter how much they produced the demand was still greater. Sugar houses sold the basic material for making alcoholic drinks, but lest someone do something improper, customers were provided with instructions on how the material could be used to make alcoholic drinks just so they would knew what to avoid doing. Sure.

As early as 1921, Hamtramck was acquiring a national reputation as a lawless town. In August 1921, the *Dearborn Independent* newspaper chronicled the situation in a story titled "The Town That Hasn't Felt the New Day" by Henry L. Commons. Commons wrote of Hamtramck:

A rough number of saloons would be 200. These saloons aren't blind pigs. Blind pigs aren't counted. We are speaking of saloons on a pre-war, pre-prohibition basis, with electric pianos and real beer. Several of these are in the same block as police headquarters. The proprietor of one of them, across the street from headquarters, shut down his electrically controlled orchestra for a time until he found out the boys on the force missed the music "something awful." Now he opens the door when customers put in a nickel in the piano, and free entertainment is afforded the police.

For many people, bootlegging was a way to make a quick buck and have a good time. But there was a much darker side to the story. Prohibition went hand in hand with prostitution, gambling and corruption, and these came to dominate much of Hamtramck as it became a city.

This was the situation that confronted Peter Jezewski as he took office as the first mayor of Hamtramck. Jezewski was a pharmacist from New York who opened a pharmacy on Jos. Campau Avenue. Ironically, the medical profession along with owning a bar have proven to be pathways to political power for Hamtramckans through the years despite their seemingly contrary character. But both professions bring the potential politician into contact with many people—people who vote.

What motivated Jezewski to move in the direction he did can only be guessed at, but certainly money and power were attractive

Peter Jezewski, a pharmacist from New York, was elected Hamtramck's first mayor in 1922. He ushered in Polish control of politics in Hamtramck that would remain nearly unbroken for seventy years.

lures, and soon he was consorting with the growing cadre of criminals in town. Among them was Chester LaMare, who become known as the "vice king of Hamtramck." LaMare operated out of his Venice Café "spaghetti restaurant" on Jos. Campau Avenue just north of Caniff Avenue (the building still stands) and was a fairly fierce gangster. He had been arrested more than eighteen times, for armed robbery, extortion and Prohibition violations. He was also believed to be involved in a host of gangland murders before he was gunned down by his own trusted aide in his Detroit home in February 1931.

Associating with such types was bound to go bad. It did. Jezewski was implicated in a scheme to haul moonshine in the city and ended up hit with a two-year sentence in Leavenworth Prison. That was more of an inconvenience than anything, and Jezewski again ran successfully for office in 1932. He wouldn't be the only Hamtramck mayor sent to prison for Prohibition violations. Mayor Rudolph Tenerowicz (a medical doctor) was not only sent to prison on Prohibition charges but also reelected mayor and then elected to Congress.

That gave an indication of what people thought of Prohibition laws. But while Prohibition was a cause of corruption, it wasn't the only sign that things were veering out of control. Gambling parlors and especially brothels were having a negative effect on the whole community. The fact that these kinds of places were able to operate so freely did not inspire confidence in the city government or police. People lost trust in their leaders and those who were supposed to be their protectors. And worse, it solidified the concept that corruption was an acceptable way of doing business. This attitude was like a cancer that spread to the school system over the next two decades. The city should have been on a track toward great prosperity, but resources often were squandered or blatantly stolen. Stories abound of building materials bought by the city or school district that were diverted to private cottages owned by officials. Jobs working for the city could be bought from officials if you were willing to pay them. For years, the common council members resisted adopting civil service, which would have made selling jobs more difficult.

All these elements came together by 1922. Hamtramck, in a sense, was a gigantic mess. The unprecedented growth in such a short time was really too much for the village council to handle. And it wasn't just them. The schools, churches and social organizations were gasping for air and room. In the space of a decade, a farming community had been transformed into an industrial city. Consider that in 1920 these were the major industries operating in the 2.1-square-mile village: Dodge Brothers, Michigan Smelting & Refining Company, Russel Wheel & Foundry Company, Michigan Radiator Company, Aluminum Casting Company, General Motors, American Electric Heater Company, Briggs Manufacturing Company, Swedish Crucible Company, Detroit Tire Carrier Company, Gear Grinding Machine Company, Michigan Steel Tube Products Company, Gordon-Weed Company, Montgomery Chemical Company and Truscon Laboratory. And this doesn't include the small machine shops and other factories that occupied small lots scattered throughout the town, often right next to residences. Zoning was virtually nonexistent. While other communities managed growth by isolating factories and having separate business districts designated through zoning, Hamtramck basically just threw everything into one big pot.

Incorporating as a city ended the animosity between the Polish and German residents, who basically gave up any power struggles. But it really didn't alter the quality of life.

Hamtramck was a city, but so what? That did nothing to alleviate the city's myriad problems. For the average Hamtramckan, incorporation meant little. They no longer had to pay township taxes, but they now had city taxes. By most accounts, life in Hamtramck was a scramble to

Jos. Campau Avenue at Yemans Street, looking south. A wide variety of businesses were opening on land that just a few years earlier had been farms.

survive. Living conditions were fairly primitive; jobs—mainly in the factories—were almost unbearable; and recreation, if you had the energy to do anything after a grueling six-day work week (reduced to five days by many businesses in 1922), was limited to picnics (for families), drinking at bars (mainly for men) and going to the movies (for everyone). Like many other towns, movie theaters were becoming popular in the late 1910s and 1920s. Farnum Theater opened in 1918 followed by Martha Washington, Campau Theater, White Star, Caniff Theater, Conant Theater and Pasttime Theater. Because of Hamtramck's large Polish population, the theaters often featured Polish movies.

The Tau Beta Community House on Hanley Street offered social activities, including dances and parties. The St. Anne's Community House on Andrus Street also offered activities on a smaller scale. Both of these organizations would expand in the coming years, especially after the start of the Great Depression in 1929, when people desperately turned to them for help. A popular distraction that existed well into the age of television was porch-sitting. During hot summer months, when no one had air conditioning,

Conditions were rather rough in the early days of the Jaworski Meat Market on Jos. Campau Avenue.

families would gather on porches. And because the houses in Hamtramck are so close together, it was easy to communicate with neighbors. Those who felt a little more restless would walk down the blocks, stopping and talking with neighbors along the way. It might seem trivial today, when people are addicted to TV or the internet, but those interactions helped reinforce the sense of community. Knowing your neighbor is an important step in maintaining a neighborhood.

Even before the Russian Revolution in 1917, socialism and communism were grabbing the public's attention. In April 1912, noted socialist Edward McGurty came to Hamtramck to deliver a lecture on the benefits of socialism. The Russian Revolution and toppling of the czar resonated here because of the focus on the plight of workers at that time. The communists stood up against the capitalist industrialists, demanding better pay and working conditions for workers. Further, they said there should be no discrimination based on race or gender. This was especially appealing to the fledgling factory worker unions that often were fighting for the same things the communists were promoting. The blending of interests blurred the lines of politics, and persons who might never accept communism in another context found themselves attracted to it because of the shared human rights principles.

The International Workman's Hall was built on Yemans Street just east of Jos. Campau Avenue, and until the 1950s, when the movement largely fell out of favor, the building hosted numerous rallies, speeches, movie presentations and other activities. It couldn't really be considered entertainment, but it certainly offered a contrast to the drudgery of day-to-day living. And politics aside, the communists had a point. Non-unionized workers at that time had little to say about working conditions. The managers could increase hours without explanation, and if a worker complained, he (or she) could be fired on the spot. The litany of injustices workers had to endure could fill more than one book and has. While the immigrants in Hamtramck had a higher tolerance level because so many were just glad to have a job in America, even they had limits. That would be more reflected in the next decade. But in 1922, the job market was still tight despite the opening of so many factories. Even the expansion of Dodge Main with the construction of an eight-story 500,000-square-foot manufacturing building expected to employ several hundred additional employees did not ease the tension among the working class. Life was still precarious for many people. They desperately needed jobs. Social services were scarce, especially for families, who had to pay rent or a mortgage, buy food, dress the kids and have the necessities to survive. Without a job and steady income, the threat of becoming homeless was real. From time to time, the city learned that some homeless folks had moved into the voting shacks that were used during elections. These small, portable structures were erected at places around town on election day because Hamtramck's population was so great that elections had huge turnouts, necessitating having more places to vote. But between elections, the shacks were stored behind Keyworth Stadium. Of course, there was no water, electricity or toilets, but they did provide shelter. At least until the squatters were ousted by the police.

In many ways, life could be primitive, if not brutal. Newspaper reports of suicides were common. Excessive drinking remained a problem despite Prohibition and the supposed closing of all saloons. And things were about to get a whole lot worse. For while Hamtramck was bustling with prosperity, the economic floor of the city—and the nation—was about to collapse with the coming of the Great Depression. The timing couldn't have been worse. The city's population was approaching fifty-six thousand, and there were thirty major factories operating in town as the decade came to a close.

Prohibition brought a new level of corruption to town. Bootlegging, gambling and prostitution flourished. Periodically, city officials and the police would put on public displays of how they were cleaning up the town. That all amounted to nothing.

Seems like the scenario for success, but on October 29, 1929—Black Tuesday—the Stock Market crashed. In fact, it didn't crash; it was decimated. There had been signs of trouble going back nearly two months, but few outside of Wall Street could have envisioned the chaos that was to come. To the average Hamtramckan, the very concept of owning stock was hard to comprehend. Yet this economic collapse would have devastating effects on Hamtramck. Businesses would close and workers were laid off. The unemployment rate in Michigan hit 52 percent, and it was even higher in Hamtramck. Auto production plummeted by two-thirds between 1929 and 1932. That affected the auto supplier too, so in quick order, the city was awash with people growing more desperate by the day. They turned to the city for aid. In 1934, newly elected mayor Joseph Lewandowski was pressed on why the city couldn't or wouldn't do more to help. "Every factory was closed," Lewandowski said. "The people couldn't pay their taxes." He said he asked the city treasurer John Anger how much money was in the city's treasury. The answer was stunning: "Seventy-eight cents."

EXPERIENCE IT

Go to the far north end of the city on the east side of Jos. Campau. Just before Carpenter Street, look down at the sidewalk and see one cracked slab that carries the imprint of Peter Plewa and the year it was installed, 1922.

IN THE NEWS

5-CENT BREAD FIRM BLOWN UP BY RIVALS IN DETROIT

DETROIT—Jan. 26.—A terrific bomb explosion in the doorway of the Warsaw bakery, Hamtramck, threw scores of citizens from their beds, slightly injuring two and doing a property damage of $20,000. The explosion is said by David Rosen, proprietor of the bakery, to have been the work of rival bakeries who objected to the Warsaw Company selling bread at 5 cents a loaf.

—Washington Times, *January 26*

DODGE LOST $12,500 SHAKING GOLD DICE

DETROIT—In a game with gold dice played in a Hamtramck saloon John Duval Dodge lost $12,500, it was revealed in a suit filed to-day in Circuit Court against Dodge and Al Day, boxing referee, by Nick Frank.

Frank says Dodge lost the money to Day. The referee in turn gave Frank a check for $10,000 signed by Dodge in payment for stock in the Frank Products Company. When Frank tried to cash the check he found that Dodge had stopped payment. Another $2,500 check signed by Dodge was cashed by Day immediately after the game.

Dodge says Day's dice and the game were not fair. Day says gold dice furnished by Dodge were used.

—New York Herald, *May 23*

"VILLAGE" OF HAMTRAMCK SEEKS TO ANNEX PART OF DETROIT

DETROIT—Hamtramck, the "village" with a population of 48,000, completely surrounded by the city of Detroit, and which has refused to become part of Detroit, seeks to annex a part of this city. The Hamtramck Republican Club today announced plans to put before the voters in November, a proposal to annex a foreign quarter with a population of 50,000. Citizens of Polish descent comprise 80 percent of Hamtramck's population and the same percentage of that nationally was shown by the 1920 census to reside in the Detroit area it has proposed to annex.

—Evening Star, *February 23*

5

1935

THE DIARY OF DORIS

TUESDAY, JANUARY 1—Happy New Year! Let's all step out and celebrate. And let's hope it is better than last year. Tomorrow is my eighteenth birthday—and I can hardly wait. Momma has not said a word, but I know she hasn't forgotten. This is just too big. In just a few months, I will be graduating from Hamtramck High, and I will be able to go out into the world on my own. Well, we will see. I think I might try to get a job first. We sure could use the money. But I will get one as soon as I can. It's just so hard to find anything. I'm still doing babysitting, but that doesn't pay anything. And I hate those little monsters I take care of. If I only had a car. But I don't have a driver's license. Just too much to think of. I'm just going to concentrate on my schoolwork. Who knows, maybe I will get a scholarship and go to college. Maybe Tommy and I will get married. But I don't know. I don't want to get stuck like Momma. She's great. So is Papa, but it seems like their life is nothing but work and worrying. Always it's about money or Papa's job. I want to do things. I want to see the world. Maybe I can go to Hollywood and become a movie star. Tommy says I am pretty. That's all I need.

THURSDAY, JANUARY 3—I was right. Momma did have a birthday cake for me. And it was one that she bought from the bakery. She bakes great cakes, of course, but one from the bakery is special. And Momma and Papa bought me a new dress as a gift. They're going to have a Midwinter

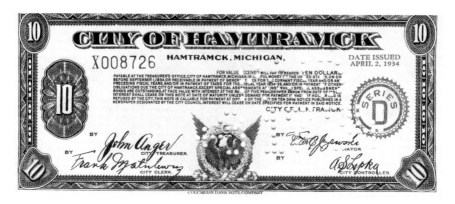

During the Great Depression, cash was short. Hamtramck, like many other towns across the country, printed its own currency from 1932 to 1934.

Carnival later this month at Kanas Hall on Conant. I think I will wear it and go there, if I can get Tommy to buy tickets. He better. He would have forgotten my birthday altogether if I hadn't reminded him a million times. And he still only gave me a box of candy and some flowers. And I'm pretty sure he picked the flowers from our neighbor's yard. Well, at least he tried. He isn't working either except when he can get some job cleaning up and things like that at the local stores on the weekends. He hasn't got much either. My brother Bobby gave me a card he made himself. He's only twelve and doesn't have any money so I was happy just to get the card. My best friend Alice gave me a new pair of gloves. That was really nice of her, but I think they are gloves that someone had given her. But that was still nice.

SATURDAY, JANUARY 5—Mister Maksimowicz killed himself. I can't believe it. He was only thirty years old. He lived just down the street from us, and I saw him just the other day. He seemed ok, but Papa said he was very sad since he lost his job. He just couldn't get another one, and he was living with his Momma. He shot himself and his Momma found him. I just can't believe that someone could feel that bad to do that. I guess that things like that just happen, but it is so sad.

SUNDAY, JANUARY 6—It was really cold, but it still was a great day. Tommy and I took the streetcar and went to Belle Isle, where we went ice skating. Lots of people were out on the ice. I'm really tired, but it sure was a lot of fun. I'd like to go again next week.

TUESDAY, JANUARY 8—They picked the school motto. It's "Excelsior Forever." What does that mean? What kind of motto is that? That's dumb.

Stanley Zieminski's corner store was typical of the time. Such stores were anchors on nearly every street corner.

Our flower is the talisman rose, and our colors are coral pink and lotus blue. Those are ok, I guess. And I suppose it doesn't matter much anyway. I'm just nervous. I want to be out of school, but then what?

WEDNESDAY, JANUARY 9—A new store is going to open up on Jos. Campau. It's called Johnny's Variety Store, and they said it will have all kinds of dresses and stockings and stuff like that. And they're promising to give a gift to every new customer. I hope so because I can't buy much. Those brats I'm supposed to babysit for the neighbor both came down with something, and their Momma had to stay home and take care of them. They should be ok, though. They have plenty of energy. At least when I'm around. They are constantly getting into trouble. I don't think I'll ever have kids. They are just too much trouble.

FRIDAY, JANUARY 11—When I got up this morning, it was freezing in the house. We ran out of coal for the furnace. This is a big problem because we don't have much money. Papa's hours at the factory have been cut again, and it's hard for us to pay all the bills. But we have to get the heat going again. Papa said if we don't, the water pipes will freeze and break and then we will really have an even bigger problem. I went to school, where at least it was warm, but I was so scared coming home because I didn't know what to expect. But I was glad when I came in and it was warm again. Papa said he managed to get enough coal to last at least until payday because he knows a guy at the coal yard. Bobby got a wagon and went to the rail yards, where he managed to find some loose coal lying around. He brought that home and said he would go out every day to look for more until spring. Tommy said I could always come and stay at his house, but I don't think his parents would approve. And neither would mine. I'm going to see if I can find a real job. I don't want to quit school because I'm so close to graduating, but I think the next six months are going to be really hard. I'm starting to get really scared.

TUESDAY, JANUARY 15—Papa said he heard some good news. He said he heard that the city is going to ask the federal government for money to do a bunch of projects in the city, including making St. Francis Hospital bigger. If they get the money that will mean more jobs will open up. He might be able to get some work there. With his hours cut back at the factory, he has time to do other work.

FRIDAY, JANUARY 18—Got some bad news from Mrs. Rybelski. She is the Momma of the two kids I babysit. It looks like they may have polio. They are eight and ten, and both of them are really sick, Mrs. Rybelski said. She is really upset. Both kids were moved to a hospital in Detroit. Now I'm worried if I got polio. After all, I've been with them a lot, but I don't feel sick at all, so maybe I'm worrying for nothing.

SATURDAY, JANUARY 19—Tommy and I double dated with Alice and her boyfriend Henry and went to a dance at the YWCA hall on the Boulevard and Dubois this evening. It was nice. There were a lot of people there.

The backyard of a typical home was cluttered and cramped. Laundry was hung outdoors, and there was an outhouse in the barn out back.

THE BIRTHDAY BALL

FOR THE

PRESIDENT

JANUARY 30, 1935

AT THE

HAMTRAMCK HIGH SCHOOL

The birthday of President Franklin Roosevelt was celebrated across the country in 1935. A big party was held in honor of the president at Hamtramck High School.

Maybe two hundred. And the hall was decorated very nice, but the weather was awful. Rain and snow. But the band playing there was good. They were called the Happy Varsity Boys. I never heard of them before. But it did make me feel happy for a while.

Friday, January 25—I can't believe it. The newspaper said that they are planning to have 5,600 birthday parties for President Roosevelt. I don't know where they all will be held, but I know one will be at the high school on January 30. I know because I saw some guys working on a big project in the school gym. I asked a worker what he was doing, and he said they are building a copy of the White House—seventy feet long—that they are going to place against one of the walls for the big party. Wow! Papa and Momma like President Roosevelt a lot. Papa says he cares about the working man, but I'm not sure how. Anyway, I don't think I'll be going to this party because it's going to be filled with city big shots and that means there will be expensive tickets to get it. I don't really care. There are dances around here all the time, and that's good enough for me.

Monday, January 28—The new semester at school started today. About the most interesting thing is that the new freshmen from Copernicus school came for their first day at Hamtramck High School. They looked so lost. I didn't go to ninth grade at Copernicus because it hadn't been built yet so my classes were in the high school building. Transferring to high school was easy for me. But everything is new for these kids. But they will get used to it. If they're smart (I'm sure they are not) they will get involved in some of the activities here. I'm a member of the Forensics Society, and I take public speaking classes. I figure they may help me if I go to Hollywood and become a movie star. I just wish they had acting classes. But I'm pretty good at acting anyway. You should hear the stories I tell my teachers when I'm late for class.

Friday, February 1—Went to the movies with Tommy. Saw something called *The St. Louis Kid* with James Cagney at the Martha Washington. It was ok. Nothing special. But next week they are going to have a Douglas Fairbanks movie called *The Private Life of Don Juan*. Some folks say he is over the hill, but I still think he is aces. I'm going to make Tommy take me to see this one. If he won't go, I'm going to see it with Alice.

Thursday, February 7—It looks like Papa is going to get some extra work. This city is going to hire 150 men to clear the snow off the streets. They already have 200 men doing that, but after the heavy snowfall we had they need more. But there is a catch. No one is going to get paid until March. The city said they won't have enough money to pay them before then. But at least it's something to look forward to. Papa went to the city council meeting Wednesday afternoon and said that there were about 100 men there looking for the jobs. He applied too. We need to do something soon. I'm going to start seriously looking for a job.

Friday, February 8—I came home from school today and found Momma crying. She tried to hide it from me, but I could tell she was crying. She didn't want to tell me, but it looks like Papa is going to be laid off from his job. That means we will have no money. Now I know I have to go to work. Not too far from here I saw the stuff people owned piled on the sidewalk. They had been evicted. I don't know what they are going to do, but I don't want to end up like them. Momma said she asked the city about getting welfare, and I know that would just kill Papa if we had to do that. But they told her there wasn't any money for that anyway. And we didn't qualify because she and Papa only have two children and I'm eighteen now. Tomorrow she's going to go over to the Tau Beta house and see if they can help. They do a lot of good things for people. We'll see.

TUESDAY, FEBRUARY 12—Momma, Papa, Bobby and me sat at the kitchen table today after dinner to talk about what we are going to do. Papa said the most important thing is for me to finish high school. He said I only have a few more months to go and maybe I can get a job on the weekends. Bobby is only twelve so he can't get a real job, but he can get a paper delivery route. He said he is all for that. Momma said she is going to try to get a job too even if it is just doing laundry. Every penny we get will help. Papa also is looking for a new job, but the chances of getting that are small. Yet there's been some good news from the auto companies. They said sales of cars are going up again, and that may mean more work. And the city said that the county had approved a project to build a viaduct on Conant Avenue at the railroad tracks. They will need a lot of workers for that. Papa is so smart. He knows how to face a problem and figure out how to fix it. He said if we all pitch in, we will get through this, and things will get better. And he said that when I am a movie star none of us will have to worry about money anymore. He can still make me laugh.

MONDAY, FEBRUARY 18—Mrs. Rybelski's son died of polio, but it looks like her daughter is going to survive but likely will be paralyzed. Sometimes I wonder how life can be so cruel. Why do good people have to suffer so much when they didn't do anything wrong? Especially a kid. I feel so bad for Mrs. Rybelski and her husband, and I feel bad for saying bad things about the kids. Maybe they were brats, but all kids are sometimes.

THURSDAY, FEBRUARY 21—They had the funeral for the Rybelskis' son Casimir at St. Florian. It was heartbreaking. He was only eight. There weren't a lot of people there. It made me feel so bad. Everyone was crying. This is such a terrible thing. His sister Marie is ten, and she seems to be alright so far. At least they are saying she likely isn't going to die, but she will be sick for a long, long while and be crippled for the rest of her life. I guess I shouldn't feel so sorry for myself. Some people have things a lot worse.

MONDAY, FEBRUARY 25—Well I did it. I got a job at Graham's clothing store on Jos. Campau. It will be after school and on Saturdays. That doesn't leave me much time for any kind of fun, and even doing my homework is going to be hard. But I spoke to my teachers at school today, and they all said they understand my situation and they will try to help me. They all said they want me to graduate too.

SATURDAY, MARCH 2—We just learned that the city is going to provide medicine to protect people from pneumonia. It will be available to poor people for free. All they have to do is ask for it at the city offices. That is good.

Papa hasn't been feeling well lately and has been coughing a lot. He said he is going to get some. I hope this helps.

FRIDAY, MARCH 9—Well, the Cosmos are all wet. The team got beat Friday by Northwestern High School. That means they are out of the running for the championship. The Cosmos were leading for most of the game, but Northwestern came up from behind and won 19–18. So sad. Oh, well, there's always next year. I won't be in school, but I will always be a Cosmos.

SUNDAY, MARCH 12—We got into a discussion about food today after dinner. Momma said it's getting harder and harder to buy enough food for all of us and that it seems like prices are going up all the time even though there are more poor people than ever. I told Momma that my friend Alice said that someone came to the city council last week to complain that the big dairies in Detroit got together to fix the prices, and that's why they are so high. Doing that is illegal, she said. Milk is twelve cents a quart now. Just a little while ago, it was eleven cents a quart, and the farmers who sell the milk to the dairies said they only charge eight cents a quart. I took enough arithmetic classes in school to know that is a big jump. Maybe the city will do something about that. We're not starving, but I don't think I have had a cake from the bakery since my birthday.

THURSDAY, APRIL 4—Wow. Mr. Keyworth was elected state superintendent of schools. That's a big jump from being the Hamtramck school boss. I don't know for sure what all of this means, but it's a pretty big thing because that's all they are talking about at school. But I guess that means he will be leaving Hamtramck. Too bad. I think our schools have been pretty good to me except for a few crumbs I have met.

WEDNESDAY, APRIL 10—This is a real gasser. The guy who runs the Premier Dairy on Jos. Campau got arrested. Guess why. He let a cat walk across tubs of butter and macaroni on display at the place. The owner was arrested for selling unsanitary stuff, and even the cat spent the night in jail until he was taken to the dog pound the next day. And yet they charge so much for milk. That beats all!

THURSDAY, APRIL 18—This is harder than I thought it would be. Trying to manage work and school is really tough. That's why there is such a big gap between my entries in this diary. Sometimes when I get home from work after being in school all day, I am so exhausted all I want to do is go to bed. I am going to do that now.

SUNDAY, APRIL 28—Happy Easter. We all went to St. Florian Church today for Mass. It was packed, but it always is. We had a nice dinner too. Not much special but at least we had something.

Dances were a major form of entertainment in the 1920s and 1930s. They were held at halls in and around the city.

TUESDAY, MAY 7—Mother's Day is coming up, and I don't know what to do. I don't have any money. I already give her and Papa almost everything I make working at the store now. I don't have anything left for me. The Metropolitan Club is sponsoring a Mother's Day dance, and I don't know how much tickets are yet, but I'd like to get them for her and Papa. Of course, Papa is such a cement mixer, he can't dance more than two steps without tripping. But it would be nice for them to go out together.

FRIDAY, MAY 10—They are going to build a new post office in Hamtramck. I read about it in the newspaper today. I wonder if I could get a job with the post office. I don't want to deliver letters, but maybe there is some kind of office job I could get. I can type, and I'm really good at spelling.

MONDAY, MAY 13—I got lucky. Florian Greenhouse by St. Florian Church was sponsoring a contest. All you had to do was go to the place and look around. They gave everyone who came a raffle ticket. I got one, and it turned out to be one of three they picked in a special drawing. The winners got free flowers delivered to their house on Mother's Day. I won, and Momma got

The Ladies Auxiliary of the Metropolitan Club was one of the many social organizations that flourished throughout the twentieth century. The Metropolitan Club was made up of firefighters, police officers and mail carriers.

her flowers. She was slap happy and so surprised she couldn't talk. She cried again, but this time it was for something good.

SATURDAY, MAY 18—Today was prom day at HHS. I wore the dress Momma and Papa bought me for my birthday. I went with Tommy, and we had a great time. This was my last prom. And it was out of this world even though it was held in the boys' gym at school. For the whole evening, I forgot about everything else. I just wanted to have fun, and I did. Benny Kyte and Golden Tower Orchestra played, and the place was filled with snazzy decorations. But now as I am getting ready for bed I am wondering where I am going in my life. This year has been so bad I want to cry when I think of all the things I have missed. I really wanted to be in the school play. It was *Along Came Peggy*, and it looked like a lot of fun. But I couldn't be in it. I couldn't get off from work for rehearsals. It broke my heart, but I guess I never was really serious about being an actress. I'm not going to Hollywood. I just don't want to be stuck in this house. I love Momma and Papa and Bobby, but I feel trapped. I feel like I'll never make enough money to get out on my own, and I'm afraid to marry Tommy or anyone else. I want more than working in a store on Jos. Campau. I want to go to college, but even if I got a scholarship, I have to work to help support the family. I tried to talk to Tommy about this, but when I bring it up he gets all bent and turns into a twit. I talk with Alice about this, but she's in the same spot. She doesn't know what to do either. I'm really tired, but I don't think I'm going to sleep well tonight.

THURSDAY, JUNE 6—It's done. Today was graduation day. I was one of 456 kids to graduate from Hamtramck High School. I suppose I shouldn't say kids because we're not kids anymore. Mr. Keyworth gave us our diplomas. They said we were the biggest graduating class in the history of the school. Momma and Papa wanted to have a party for me, but we just couldn't do it They said they would make it up to me someday, but I told them not to worry about it.

WEDNESDAY, JUNE 12—Now that I am out of school, I can start working full time. That will bring in more money for the family. But I am also going to use some time to find a better job. I heard that Auto City Brewery is going to expand their plant in Hamtramck. That's not far from where we live. I could walk there. I'm going to see if I can get in there. But I'm also going to look at some of the downtown stores. The streetcar company said it is going to improve service to Hamtramck. That should make getting downtown easier.

SUNDAY, JUNE 23—Everyone is in shock. Mr. Keyworth has died. He was killed in a car crash yesterday Up North. He was just elected state school superintendent and was visiting some schools there when his car was hit head-on by another car. He was taken to a hospital and died a short time later. I can't believe it. I just got my diploma from him a couple weeks ago. Now he is gone. I don't know what else to say.

TUESDAY, JUNE 25—They had a big ceremony for Mr. Keyworth at the high school yesterday and today. I went to it. I think there were thousands of people there. It was huge. All kinds of speakers praised what a great man he was. They brought his body to the school where it is laid in state in the gym. It was the biggest funeral I ever saw. They are supposed to be taking his body up to Gaylord now to be buried. He was from there. I'm not even sure where that is.

THURSDAY, JULY 25—Haven't been writing too much, at least here. But I have been very busy. Business is picking up and we are pretty busy at the store. Things have gotten a little better for Papa too. He got called back to work and is bringing in a steady income now. It's still not as much as

Even though times were tough during the Great Depression, people did their best to modernize their homes, buying the latest appliances when they could afford them.

before, but it is better. Things have definitely improved, but I still am not satisfied. I still want to do something better.

FRIDAY, AUGUST 2—I can't believe how bananas things have gotten in the last week. There's been talk around town for a while about the cost of food. Well some women have formed a group called the Hamtramck Committee for Action Against the High Cost of Living (I think I got that right). Well, they had a big rally in a lot across from Copernicus school where about four hundred women protested against the cost of meat. Mary Zuk, who I was told was a communist, gave a rip snortin speech and fired up the crowd. They went on a parade to some of the local meat markets where they raised a lot of noise. I heard they even bought meat and threw it in the street. They started a boycott saying no one should buy any meat. Mrs. Zuk said if they keep up the fight, they will cut the cost on meat by 20 percent. I don't know about that. Anyway, I can't believe it, but Momma went to the rally and even marched in the parade. She never would do anything like that before. She's becoming a fighter. But I can't help smiling because she sure doesn't look like a fighter.

THURSDAY, AUGUST 8—The fight is going onward. Last night a bunch of the local butchers held a big meeting in the hall on McDougall and Holbrook. They said they will not cut the cost of meat even if the boycott continues. They said that the Depression and the drought out west is causing the rising prices, and they can't do anything about it. And now the meat strike is spreading. There have been pickets at meat markets in Detroit and Lincoln Park. Mostly it's been peaceful, but a few of the women were arrested. I told Momma she better not get arrested, and I wasn't going to bail her out if she did. Of course, I would. She just laughed, but she is serious about fighting for lower prices.

SATURDAY, AUGUST 17—Finally some good news. Tommy got hired to be part of the crew that will build the new viaduct on Conant. Work is supposed to begin in a few weeks, and the job is expected to take until next spring to complete. The city said only Hamtramck residents were being hired for the job. Now he can take me to more dances and maybe even to a restaurant once in a while.

SATURDAY, AUGUST 31—The meat strike continues, and Momma is really getting active with them. Yesterday she was making signs that said "Don't Buy Meat" and stuff like that. The butchers tried to get the police to stop the picketers, but they haven't been able to, at least not yet. And the cost of meat is still high.

FRIDAY, SEPTEMBER 13—I read in the paper that 2,500 families on welfare now will be getting jobs through the government WPA program. But another 500 families will stay on welfare. I don't understand it all, but apparently if there is a problem with the WPA program, and there are a lot of congressmen who are against it, the city could get stuck with taking care of all 3,000 families. That's a lot of people, and the city can't afford it. Right now we can't get help from the city, and if the WPA program doesn't happen it could get even worse for us. Always something new to worry about.

SATURDAY, SEPTEMBER 21—It's been quiet lately. Momma hasn't been out picketing for days, and it looks like the meat strike is fading away. I went with Tommy to the movies to see *Broadway Gondolier* at Martha Washington. It was ok I guess. Dick Powell did a lot of singing. I liked the ice cream we got after the movie a lot better than the movie.

TUESDAY, OCTOBER 8—They started building the new post office on Caniff today. That's important because it's a WPA project and seventy-five men will be needed to work on it. Anything that brings more jobs to town will help us all.

FRIDAY, OCTOBER 18—I got off from work a little early today, and I stopped by Bejnar's music store and looked at radios. They have a wonderful one on sale for sixty dollars. It's beautiful and it can get everything, even police calls. I really like to listen to the Jack Benny program. He is so funny. It's a beautiful radio, but of course, I can't get it. It's just too expensive. Well, maybe someday…

MONDAY, OCTOBER 28—Shopping has picked up, and we are getting even more customers at the store. If this keeps up, I am going to ask for a raise. I'm sure I won't get it, but I am going to try. The merchants have started a Merchants Prosperity Campaign to generate more business. They are giving away prizes including cash and things on sale. One woman at Norman Lee's store won a pair of stockings. I think I'm going to enter.

FRIDAY, NOVEMBER 1—Alice and I are going to the Martha Washington tomorrow evening. Tommy has to work late, and we want to hear the new sound system that has been installed in the theater. They say it makes it sound like the person in the movie is sitting right next to you. Not sure about the movie. It's called *Annapolis Farewell* and sounds like it's about the navy. It stars Sir Guy Standing. Sir? Is he some kind of English knight? I never heard of him. But it's got to be better than sitting at home.

THURSDAY, NOVEMBER 28—Today is Thanksgiving. I have to admit it could have been worse. Momma and Papa invited Aunt Caroline and her family to come over for dinner. They brought food with them, so we had a fairly nice meal. Aunt Caroline even brought over a big box of candy she got at Bardy's Confectionary. Bobby really liked that. Papa and Uncle Bob each had a bottle of beer. They really liked that too.

FRIDAY, NOVEMBER 29—An interesting thing happened at the store today. A man came in to buy a dress for his wife's birthday. We got into a conversation, and he told me he worked at a business downtown that was looking for a reliable clerk to help out with things. He asked if I was interested in applying for the job. He said they paid pretty good. I told him I wasn't trained to be a secretary, but I can type. He said that didn't matter, just so long as I was reliable. After he left, I looked up the place in the phone book and they were listed. I'm going to call Monday and see if I can apply for the job.

TUESDAY, DECEMBER 10—I had my job interview. It seemed to go well. From what I can see, I can do what they want, and the pay is way better than the store. Of course, I will have to take the streetcar, but it's right downtown so it won't be a bad trip except maybe in winter. But who knows, if things go well, I may get a car. Although that will mean I will have to learn how to drive. But how hard can that be to learn? They said they would contact me in a couple days to let me know if I get the job.

FRIDAY, DECEMBER 13—Well, this sure wasn't a bad Friday the 13th, at least as far as shopping. It has been completely bats all over Jos. Campau. People are everywhere. My boss said the stores are having the best Christmas season since the bottom fell out of the stock market. Maybe I'll get a Christmas bonus.

WEDNESDAY, DECEMBER 25—Merry Christmas! Lots to say but I am going to wait another week.

TUESDAY, DECEMBER 31—This is going to be my last entry to this diary and my last entry ever. No, this is not a bad thing. In fact, I'm not sure how to take all of this. But I got the job and so far I love it. But what I really like is the money. I hate to admit it, but it has made such a difference. I not only can help Momma and Papa I have some left over for me. First thing I did was buy a bakery cake for Christmas. We didn't have one last year. Then I bought Bobby a Christmas present, a baseball and glove. He actually cried when he unwrapped it. So did I. As I am writing this now it really is no longer 1935. It's 1:15 a.m. on January 1, 1936. And this is the last thing I want to do before I go to bed. It's been a hard year, the hardest of my life so far. But I am looking ahead to the new year with hope and with an understanding that we all are a lot tougher than I thought. I think Momma and Papa, Papa especially, knew that all along. Papa never seemed to be beaten down, even in the worst days. He seemed to know we would make it. We are not out of trouble yet, but I think we are going to be ok. As for me, I know acting is a dream that has ended. I'm awake now, and I have to face reality. But I also know that reality is what I make it. I'm going to do very well at this job, and by the time I am through I may own the company. I am looking forward to the future. That's why I am closing out this diary forever. Diaries are accounts of the past. Now I am looking ahead.

Experience It

Visit the Hamtramck Post Office on Caniff at the corner of Mitchell Street. Read the cornerstone that was placed there when the building was dedicated in 1935, and then go inside and look at the WPA murals on the lobby walls. Also, go by the PLAV hall at Holbrook and McDougall Streets. This hall hosted innumerable dances through the years.

In the News

Preliminary Cleanup Plans to Be Discussed by Committee

Members of civic organizations and Hamtramck Municipal department heads are to meet today at 10 a.m. to discuss preliminary plans for the annual Cleanup Campaign which is to take place early in May. The city will be striving to win for the eighth consecutive time the cup given by the National committee to the city making the best progress during the campaign based on reports.

—New Deal, *March 24*

Children Given Own Camp Site

Hamtramck Children now have their own outdoor camp! Such was the gift received by the children this week when Mrs. Josephine Clay Kanzler, Tau Beta Camp Chairman, turned over to a general camp committee 106 beautiful acres of forest and streams.

—New Deal, *May 17*

Hamtramck to Have Joe Louis Day

The Hamtramck City Council at a special meeting held Tuesday morning designated July 19, 1935, as "Joe Louis Day" in the city of Hamtramck by action of a resolution proposed by Councilman Joseph J. Mitchell and supported by Councilman Walter Kanar.

—Tribune Independent of Michigan, *July 6*

Sunday Closings Protested

The Common Council is going to meet with the Butcher's and Grocer's Association as soon as possible to decide whether or not the city fathers will remove from the City Charter "an ordinance which they do not even try to enforce." The ordinance under fire is the regulation which requires all Hamtramck butchers and grocers to keep their stores closed on Sunday.

—The Citizen, *September 27*

6

1945

The folks at White House Cleaners and Dryers took steps to honor their customers. Jean Wieczynski was one. She was a "war wife."

Like so many other women at the time, she had adapted, as much as possible, to the reality that she had a loved one away and at war. For her, it was her husband, Corporal William Wieczynski, who was in the Pacific theater of operations. In January 1945, she was "waiting and hoping for the end of the war so that her husband can come home."

That's the way the ad in *The Citizen* newspaper framed it in the edition of January 19, 1945. The ad promoted White House Cleaners and Dryers, at 10026 Jos. Campau, as part of its Guest of the Week feature. Such promotions were common at the time to pay tribute to soldiers and their families "in the spirit of friendship." It also noted that Mrs. Wieczynski "gets into war work herself, sewing parachutes at the National Automotive Fibres plant where she has been employed for two years."

The Wieczynskis had been married for four years, and William had been in the service for three of those years. His three brothers—Ray, Dick and Ed—also were in the military.

By this time, the war had become a way of life. It seemed to dominate everything. All facets of life had been affected by the conflict. World War II hit Hamtramck hard, going back to September 1, 1939, when Germany invaded Poland. Although the United States was not involved at that time, many Hamtramckans were Polish or of Polish descent and had close relatives still living—and now dying—in Poland. Here folks hung Hitler in effigy on Jos. Campau. Some went to Canada to join the army there so they could fight for their former homeland. Many others contributed to the numerous fundraisers that were held to support Poland. While the United States was gearing up for war long before the attack on Pearl Harbor, to the Poles, the war had already begun. In fact, it had begun even before the first shots were fired. In April 1939, the Stop Dictators committee was formed in Hamtramck to devise ways to raise money to help Poland counter the growing Nazi threat. Organizers of the committee appeared before the common council and were enthusiastically supported.

But in reality, there was little they could do. Officially, the United States was neutral, so certain activities, like sending weapons to a warring county, were illegal. That all changed on December 7, 1941, with the attack on Pearl Harbor. And it was as if a dam had burst. Suddenly, organizations and activities related to the war effort were sparked.

In January 1942, the new Hamtramck Civilian Defense Council was formed to deal with wartime matters. For example, it solicited women to volunteer for the Hamtramck Red Cross Motor Corps. "Registrants must be at least 18 years of age, physically fit, and willing to learn the actual handling of cars and practical knowledge, in the meaning of minor repairs, in keeping motor vehicles in proper running order," the council noted.

World War II affected all facets of life. Everyone cut back on essentials. Even kids acted by collecting mountains of scrap paper that would be reused.

Mayor Stephen Skrzycki goes over war bond sales with Alex Krot. The city sponsored numerous bond drives throughout the war.

At 2:00 p.m. on Sunday, January 18, 1942, the council held a community meeting at Hamtramck High School to discuss civilian defense and "just what Hamtramck is in for and what it can do about it in the way of preparation." And within a week, the Buy a Bomber campaign was in swing with volunteers going door to door seeking donations to fund the building of a bomber in Hamtramck's name. The campaign raised more than $2,000, hardly enough to "Buy a Bomber," but it was worth a million in building community spirit. And that was probably the biggest positive effect of the war. Almost everyone seemed united in their support of the war effort. Suddenly, priorities and perspectives had changed. Clyde Wishart, research and education director for the UAW-CIO, spoke at the Defense Council meeting and told the audience that "labor is cooperating 100 percent in the war effort," as reported in *The Citizen*. "Labor feels it is better to work to death defeating Hitler than to face the prospect of working for Hitler."

But the bravado was tempered with the reality that the threat of dying was fast approaching. At the same meeting, a plan was revealed to divide the city into three hundred units to respond quickly if the city were to be bombed. The Dodge Main plant at the south end of town made a tempting target, and despite the distance from Germany to Hamtramck, a bombing raid was not far-fetched. It was envisioned the bombers could fly from Germany to Norway, to Canada and down to Detroit. It may seem a bit overreaching now, but during the war, that was a plausible threat.

More Defense Council meetings would follow. Air raid drills would be held, scrap drives became common and practical pain at the home level began to be felt as rationing was implemented and shopping for food became more challenging. At the urging of the city, residents started planting Victory Gardens using even tiny plots of land to grow farm crops to supplement their pantries. The city passed Ordinance No. 188, which provided for the creation of Victory Gardens "on vacant lots and other available real estate" under the supervision of a newly created Victory Garden Commission. By March 1943, the city had identified five hundred parcels of land to be made available for the gardens and was contacting owners for their permission to use the sites.

But you couldn't grow gasoline or things like tires, so a strict rationing process was put into place. If you were fortunate enough to own a car, you had to carefully weigh where you were going to drive and how much gas that would use. So planning a dinner took greater effort and imagination, as just getting the ingredients became a challenge. People managed as best they could while maintaining a positive attitude. There is a marvelous Popeye cartoon of the period in which Olive Oyl drives her car with no tires, just shoes attached to each of the wooden spokes on the car's wheel hubs. There's no record of anyone actually trying that, but who knows?

This was war, and as the conflict deepened, the reality began to sink in. Although the draft had been reinstituted in September 1940, before the United States' entry into the war, the pace of registrations, volunteering and calls to service increased. All men between twenty-one and forty-five years old had to register for the draft, but some, such as those deemed physically or mentally unfit or those employed in essential fields, like engineers, were exempt. Fathers were also exempt, although with the wave of patriotism that arose after Pearl Harbor, many did volunteer. In fact, so many volunteered or were drafted for the service it prompted a fundamental shift in the structure of the nation and its perspective. The war became all-consuming. Virtually every aspect of society was influenced by it, especially families who had a member in the service. Husbands and boyfriends kissed wives and girlfriends goodbye for a separation that would last several years or—in some cases—forever. Try to feel the pain of uncertainty parting couples and families had at the time. No one had any idea of how long the war would last. The soldiers boarded trains in downtown Detroit taking them to training bases around the country and then to the war zone. A man who spent dreary days on the line at Dodge Main was quickly transformed into a soldier, carrying and using a weapon to try to kill other people in foreign lands. Few had any experience in that other Great War, which Americans fought in more than twenty years earlier, and not even the scope of that conflict could compare to the vastness of World War II. For some, it was a great adventure, at least at the beginning. It was a chance to visit exotic lands and experience the excitement of battle. But it often turned into a nightmare, even for the survivors.

No one was immune from the war's effects. Even children were involved. Got that pack of gum? Be sure you save the foil the stick was wrapped in. It is needed for the war effort. High school kids were not immune. In

Members of the Spirit of Hamtramck Club wrap boxes of cigarettes to be sent to soldiers overseas.

October 1942, the school board implemented a six-point program. Its goal was a lofty one—to help win the war. It included increasing the number of school courses related to war industry; pre-flight training courses for future pilots; placing more emphasis on the world situation in all subjects; pre-induction school courses to help students decide which branch of the service they would want to join; physical fitness classes; and the establishment of a Victory Corps that would engage the students in the various war efforts that were being done in the community.

How did the students react to the slate of classes? "You couldn't keep the boys and girls out of them," School Superintendent M.A. Kopka told the school board.

That month was significant for another major event but a far more ominous one. In October 1942, Corporal John Targosz, twenty, was killed when a bomb struck Henderson Field on Guadalcanal in the Pacific. The headline at the top of the front page of *The Citizen* for October 16, 1942, read "Marine Listed as City's First Casualty." Targosz had actually been killed on September 12, 1942, but the news wasn't immediately made public. He would later receive the Purple Heart. More reports of casualties would follow. In December 1942, Mr. and Mrs. John Brzozowski of Andrus Street were informed that their son, Corporal Alphonse J. Brzozowski, was killed in action in the Solomon Islands. He had been a catcher on the Hamtramck High School champion baseball team and was in the glee club. After graduating in 1940, he joined the Marines.

Blue and Gold Stars began appearing in the windows of houses everywhere. The stars were symbols awarded by the Blue and Gold Star Mothers organizations, which were formed after World War I. The Blue Star indicated that the family living in the house had a member in the service; the Gold Star indicated a family member was killed in the service.

In time, the newspaper stories of individual casualties would be gathered together in a weekly listing of items about all local veterans. "Twelve Casualties Listed among Local Servicemen" was the headline of the list in the January 5, 1945 issue of *The Citizen*. These included two killed, eight wounded and two missing. The deceased were Private Stanley Sajor, killed in the Pacific, and Private First Class Leonard A. Bury, who died in Europe.

Nothing could ease the pain of the families who lost a loved one, but the deaths became part of the fabric of everyday life. The war changed so much of daily life; to an extent, it reshaped society. Hamtramck was devastated by the Great Depression. Much of the city's population worked in factories related to the auto industry. Their jobs evaporated for the most part as the city's unemployment rate rose to an astounding nearly 60 percent. What few social services that were offered were almost immediately overwhelmed and depleted. People turned to the churches for aid, but they were crippled by the Depression as well. Weekly offerings dwindled. The Depression-era programs initiated by President Franklin Roosevelt, including the Civilian Conservation Corps and Works Progress (later Project) Administration, provided jobs to millions until employment increased as the nation prepared for the coming war.

The jobs provided welcome relief from the poverty, but as the growing war casualty list showed, this came with a terrible price. Still there was a sense of normalcy that provided a degree of comfort, especially in the latter days of the war. On June 6, 1944, the Allies successfully landed at Normandy and quickly swept inward from the coast on the way to liberating France from the Germans. The Nazis had already suffered tremendous losses in Russia, particularly in the brutal Battle of Stalingrad. As the Allies advanced across France, the hopes of victory were steadily rising. The defeat of the German counterattack in the Battle of the Bulge in December 1944 enhanced the optimism.

"A bright sign for New Year's shines brightly today from the south flank of the German offensive as reports indicate that Gen. Patton is on the rampage and lustily cracking Nazi ribs," reporter Pierre J. Huss wrote in the December 31, 1944 edition of the *Detroit Evening Times*. That was the kind of news that would buoy the spirit of a war-weary population. No one knew how much longer the war would last, especially since a prolonged battle was expected to defeat the Japanese after the Nazis were dealt with. But progress was being made.

While war-related news filled the pages of the local newspapers, other events were happening. Controversy was roiling the Hamtramck Public Schools. Charges of corruption had been raised over the illegal payment of salaries to certain board members. That led to a state audit of school assets, and the district risked losing its accreditation.

In February, a fire destroyed the Beck Shoe Store on Jos. Campau. Flames shot fifteen feet into the air above the building before the blaze was brought under control. And five thousand pairs of shoes were lost.

In March, Margaret Kuman died at age seventy-four. She and her husband, William, had come to Hamtramck in 1891 and lived in a house on Denton Street the whole time. When they came to Hamtramck, it was still mainly pastures and forests.

In May, the common council approved a $4,800 expenditure to conduct a survey of the city's leaky water system. It was expected to take three months to complete and would hopefully detect the leaks that wasted twenty million cubic feet of water annually.

In June, 450 city employees faced a payless payday when the city ran out of cash. A move to transfer money from another account to payroll was blocked by the common council, which objected to the practice of moving money from one account to another. Ultimately, after much political maneuvering, the employees were paid. Money woes continued into July, as the members of the common council refused to approve a budget put forth by the city's budget board. More political infighting ensued among the council members, City Clerk Al Zak and Mayor Stephen Skrzycki. Eventually, the matter was worked out, but it was reflective of the financial problems Hamtramck has faced virtually since it incorporated as a city in 1922, which persist to this day.

Troubles continued regarding the Col. Hamtramck Homes, which were built a few years earlier. A group of Hamtramckans had sought to have the housing project be made available only for White residents. Black Hamtramckans fought back and took the matter to court. In August, the Housing Commission proposed reserving thirty-six units for Black residents, but the matter bounced through the courts until the early 1950s, when the whole project was desegregated and open to all.

In September, nine thousand people packed Keyworth Stadium for the annual matchup between the Hamtramck High School and Catholic Central High School football squads. The weather was more suited to baseball than football, as the temperature was in the eighties. But CC was hotter than HHS and won 33–13.

Six women and three men were found guilty of frequenting a gambling establishment in a case brought before Hamtramck Justice Court in October. All but two were fined $5. The other two were fined $15. The gambling was done in a building on Caniff Street, and liquor also was available at the site. Such illegal operations remained fairly common in Hamtramck long after Prohibition ended in 1933.

Hamtramck was long the home of Dodge cars, but they weren't the only models found in town. In November, Dick Connell Chevrolet unveiled the 1946 Chevrolets, including the Stylemaster and Fleetmaster Fleet lines. "The car I've seen shows modern styling, which accentuates massiveness in smart, low, sleek lines," said Connell manager M.H. Shore.

With Christmas fast approaching, the Hamtramck Merchants' Association announced that the stores would be open from 9:30 a.m. to 9:30 p.m. daily from December 6 until Christmas. "We feel that this gives Hamtramck

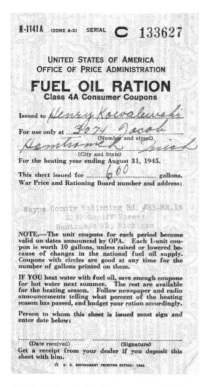

Food, fuel and drinks were extensively rationed during the war. That made life more difficult, but almost everyone wanted to pitch in.

shoppers adequate time to plan their holiday shopping and, of course, it is urged that buying be started early while stocks are complete," said Mort J. Kay, the association's advertising committee chairman.

The new Chevrolets and the increased shopping hours also demonstrated that consumer products were coming back in abundance with the end of the war.

Yet there was no letup in the pervasive influence of the war. In March 1945, William Pluto, fourteen, a Boy Scout of St. Ladislaus Troop 145, won praise for collecting seventy-five pounds of fat that could be used in the production of bullets for soldiers. He got the fat from his neighbors who did the cooking. At the same time, Chester Antoniewicz, Yeoman, Second Class, was named the Yank of the Week by Dave Stober. Antoniewicz was on leave from service in the South Pacific when he was cited by Stober. The Yank of the Week was a marketing tool that Stober used to generate publicity for his popular men's clothing store at 9438 Jos. Campau. (He would later move next to Max's Jewelry store at the corner of Jos. Campau and Belmont Streets. His name still is visible in the tiles at the entranceway of the store, although he and the business are long gone.)

Farther down the street, at 9726 Jos. Campau, Dr. Louis Goldberg, a longtime Hamtramck optometrist, had his office. He managed to tie wearing glasses into the war effort. "Men in the service need good vision," a newspaper ad stated. "Good eyesight is an ally of exacting work, contributing to the efficiency and wide awake alertness....Whether precision war worker, clerk or office worker, the condition of your eyes determines your efficiency on the job." All this was written next to the drawing of a soldier wearing glasses.

Progressive Cleaners, another longtime Hamtramck business, noted in an Easter newspaper ad: "We greet you this Easter with bright hope in our

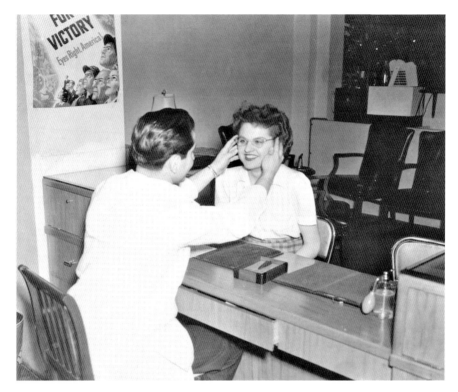

Even getting glasses was given a patriotic spin during the war. Workers who saw better worked better. Dr. M. Schwartz delivered that message along with a new pair of glasses to Wanda Paremski at Max's Jewelry store.

hearts and a resolution to carry through as before…serving the nation to the best of our abilities." Even Hank's Bar on Conant Avenue managed to deliver a war message in a newspaper ad: "The weight of war days and all their attendant unhappiness can't keep Americans down. Gather up what's left of the 'Gang' and make it an evening."

Not to be outdone, Leo Rau, who ran the popular House of Rau, lured "war workers" with the promise of dancing "from 7 a.m. to ??" "Come in your working clothes, but don't empty your pockets—They will do that before you leave." Who "they" are isn't specified.

Looking for a more passive form of entertainment? The Martha Washington Theatre was showing *A Wave, a WAC and a Marine*, in which "Anything goes, everything happens as two cuties and a fast-working boyfriend crash their way from Broadway to Hollywood before their date with Uncle Sam." It stars Elyse Knox and Ann Gillis, and before you say, "Who?" consider that the bill also includes news and a cartoon.

If you would rather stay home, you could listen to the radio. The popularity of radios soared during the war. They became a prime source of information about the progress of the war. A wide variety of entertaining programs were broadcast throughout the day, including soap operas. These would easily transfer to television just after the war ended and, ironically, killed non-music radio programming as it had been known for more than twenty-five years, going back to the start of network radio.

Not into radio? You could slip a 78-rpm record on the phonograph and hear Glenn Miller play "White Cliffs of Dover" and "When Johnny Comes Marching Home." Or you could get "Canteen Honky Tonk Boogie" by Pat Flowers. These records, and many more, were available at Bejnar's music store at 10015 Jos. Campau. They also sold washing machines, radios and musical instruments at the store.

Despite the limitations of the war, the Jos. Campau shopping strip was booming. Favorite stores, like Grant's, Kresge's and Neisner's, were as busy as ever. Margolis Furniture had "odd chests, beds and dressers" for $16.95 and up. Jack's 5th Ave. Men's Shop had "The only genuine windbreaker," which was "America's Most Famous Jacket," on sale for $8.95. Podezwa's Boot Shop was selling Poll-Parrot Arch Makers. They were sure to fit properly because the store employed that curious—and questionable— process of X-raying customers' feet to match them to the shoes. "April Brides" could still get diamond wedding rings for as little as $67.50 at Max's Jewelry. And looking ahead, baby cribs were available at Stork Lane for $12.95.

Still, the war was pervasive. Turn on the radio, and you would hear some great programs like the *Charlie McCarthy Show* and *Fibber McGee and Molly*. And almost always there would be a promo to buy war bonds.

In June 1945, Christine Wolski, a ninth grader at Copernicus Junior High School, sold $14,150 worth of war bonds to lead the entire school. In all, the school had generated $32,650 in bond sales but still had a ways to go to meet its quota of $88,000. To help spur sales, the school sponsored a king and queen contest, while a prince and princess contest was held for the elementary grades. Six-year-old Sharon Trojnarski was leading the pack for the princess title by raising $1,750 while Robert Marquette had raised $700 to become the prince.

Even as that was being held, a citywide campaign was underway to recruit women to serve as WAVES. "Hamtramck girls can be particularly useful in the hospital corps," said Alice Jane Rybicki, WAVES recruiting officer for the Hamtramck area. "The Waves are ready to train girls to do

Above: Gotta sing? Well, you could sing the words with the help of *Song Hits* magazine. This was the big band era. Gene Krupa, Vaughn Monroe, Charlie Spivak, Hal McIntyre and many more made music that could help you forget the war.

Opposite: War wasn't just for men. Ensign Helen Stewart came to Hamtramck seeking to recruit WAVES, Women Accepted for Volunteer Emergency Service.

minor surgery and first aid, prepare and administer simple medicines. An important phase of the work today is in rehabilitation centers."

To qualify, women had to be between twenty and thirty-five years old, have two years of high school or business school education, be in good physical condition and not have young children.

A milestone in the war took place in March 1944, when the Allied forces crossed the Rhine River and entered Germany. The fighting had been fierce. Staff Sergeant Vitold Dyki, who had lived on Trowbridge Street, wrote to his mother, Aniela Kowalewski, in April that there was "fighting a lot on both sides of the Rhine River." He was an extraordinarily lucky soldier. "A German rifleman shot me and the bullet went through my jacket pocket, through a spoon and cigarette case and hit a German pistol I carried over my heart, and stopped. It ruined my pistol but saved my life."

Dyki ended his letter with a telling note: "I wish all the people who think the war is over here would spend a while with us on this side of the Rhine."

His point was on target. Entering Germany signaled that the war was coming to an end in Europe. It was clear that victory was approaching, which made some overanxious. That wasn't surprising. People were war weary. Apprehension at home had grown, especially after the D-Day landing in June 1944, when Allied troops were encountering the German army directly, and as battles increased, so did casualties. More than ever, the troops were in danger, and the closer they moved toward Berlin, the more desperate the German army became.

In April 1945, Private First Class Stanley J. Rusztowicz, of Belmont Street, received the Bronze Star for bravery in laying and maintaining wiring used in communications to keep his battalion in contact with other units despite being surrounded by the enemy.

But so many more were receiving the heartbreaking telegrams informing them that their soldier wasn't coming home. Corporal Adolph Trojanowski was typical. The son of Mr. and Mrs. Casmere Trojanowski of Klinger

Street, he was wounded on March 31 fighting in Germany. He died on April 2 from his wounds. He had been in the service for two years, including ten months overseas. A 1936 graduate of Our Lady Queen of Apostles Grade School and 1940 graduate of St. Ladislaus High School, he was just twenty-three years old when he died.

Private First Class Leonard J. Smith was the same age when he was killed on March 12 at Iwo Jima. He was a seasoned veteran by then, having seen service in five major Pacific battles, including Midway, Guadalcanal and Bougainville. He was a 1940 graduate of Hamtramck High School and had enlisted in the Marines in 1942. He had received numerous medals for bravery and two presidential citations. Perhaps that provided some comfort to his family at least, knowing that he served the country honorably and bravely and he did not die in vain. Nevertheless, he was gone forever at such a young age.

Those personal tragedies were being repeated regularly as the war progressed. And despite the anticipation of the nearing end of the war in Europe, the people of Hamtramck clearly understood that this was just a step on the road to total victory.

"Hamtramck Observes V-E Day with Silence" was the lead headline on the front page of *The Citizen* on May 11, 1945. City officials had expected a big celebration when Germany surrendered. In anticipation of the surrender announcement, the local store owners said they would close on V-E Day. Morris Direnfeld, chairman of the Retailers for Victory business association, announced the planned closing but tempered the enthusiasm by noting that the war was far from over and the worst might be yet to come; the invasion of Japan would undoubtedly produce a huge number of casualties. Instead of celebrating, residents were advised to go to church and offer prayers of thanks that at least the war in Europe was over.

Another factor tempering the public mood was the recent death of President Franklin Roosevelt on April 12, 1945, less than a month before V-E Day. A memorial service for the president was being planned for June 3 at Keyworth Stadium. Hamtramck was the first city in the nation to set aside a day to pay tribute to the president. Roosevelt had been to Hamtramck in 1936 to dedicate Keyworth Stadium, which was partially funded as a Works Progress Administration project.

V-E Day arrived on Tuesday, May 8, 1945, and passed "with few outward indications that it was anything different from any other day," *The Citizen* noted. Extra policemen had been put on duty, and the sale of liquor and beer was halted. "Many factory workers poured out of plants, intent on joining the celebrations. Finding no celebrations, they went home—and stayed there."

The next day was pretty much typical for the time. Stores were open, and people went about as they had before. *The Citizen* summed up the situation:

> *Most homes…had a deeper concern—the question of when their sons, husbands and brothers would return from the silenced European fronts.*
>
> *Mayor [Stephen] Skrzycki issued a relatively lengthy proclamation calling upon the populace to join in V-E Day prayers Sunday, as requested by President Truman in his historic address Tuesday morning.*
>
> *Any victory celebration, apparently, is being held off until the remaining enemy, Japan, is defeated.*

And it was. But at a terrific price for the Japanese. On August 6, 1945, the first atomic bomb was dropped in the Japanese city of Hiroshima. Three days later, another atomic bomb was dropped on Nagasaki. On August 14, 1945, the Japanese accepted the terms for surrender.

So it was over. And this victory announcement was met quite a bit differently in Hamtramck compared to V-E Day. "Thousands of citizens poured out into the streets, with the main rush being made to Jos. Campau, where the young people cheered wildly while the older people contented themselves with watching the celebrants," *The Citizen* recounted. So many drivers sounded their vehicle horns that it was difficult to carry on a conversation in the street. People tore up newspapers to make confetti on the spot. And the stores closed through the afternoon. The burst of enthusiasm may have been enhanced because an earlier radio announcement was made that Japan had surrendered, then was retracted after questions were raised that Japan may not actually have surrendered. But then came the final word that the surrender was real. Suddenly, American flags were everywhere. They were on rows of houses along the blocks, people carried them through the streets and some were mounted on cars. Assorted Japanese military figures were hung in effigy from poles around the city, but the mood was far more upbeat than vindictive.

Police were assigned to twelve- and eighteen-hour shifts as the celebration broke out. But despite the clamor, they reported no incidents of vandalism or any crimes. The wild response was actually quite peaceful.

In all, some 7,000 Hamtramckans had served in the military during World War II. Approximately 192 died, and while each death was a tragedy, there was a sense that this was a communal loss, and in a way, they helped unite the

During and especially after the wars, veterans' groups flourished. The American Legion Post 455 was one that made an impressive appearance in parades aboard a fire truck.

community. Many veteran groups would spring up in the wake of the war, while more established groups like the Polish Legion of American Veterans would add chapters. A new sense of camaraderie grew as so many men, and to a lesser extent, women, were brought together through their shared experience of the war. An example of the growth was the attempt by the Veterans of Foreign Wars Post 4162 to establish a Veterans' Memorial Home in the old Carpenter School building on Carpenter Street in November 1945. That was one of the oldest school buildings in the city and had been annexed from the Detroit School District decades earlier. But by the 1920s, the building was considered unsafe and soon condemned. It was an unlikely site for a veterans' home and was eventually demolished.

In December, a group of Black veterans met at the city council chambers to form an organization. They were under the direction of Ordine Toliver, a Black Hamtramckan well known and respected by the whole community.

With the end of the war, the focus of everyday life began to shift. The soldiers were coming back from the service; many were getting married and looking forward to starting families. Some soldiers came home to children who were born while their fathers were away, and they were faced with young children who didn't recognize them. There were some painful periods of adjustments as the children rejected these strange men who suddenly appeared and took their mothers' attention.

By September 1945, Michigan veterans were being discharged at a rate of ten thousand per month. "It is going to tax the resources of all cities to help these men find their places in civilian life," said E.M. Conklin, counselor with the Council of American Veterans. "Veterans find many changes back home when they arrive, and they don't have much money with which to buy their clothes and other things they have to have." He went on to explain that job opportunities were available, but they were somewhat scarce. A mild recession occurred in 1945 as government spending on the war effort dropped drastically. Another recession occurred in 1948–49, but neither was especially serious, and the pent-up demand brought about by domestic shortages during the war meant there was a market for many goods, like washing machines and cars. Employment in both recessions remained relatively high, and soon the Dodge Main factory was making cars again.

But as the war ended, another casualty became apparent: Hamtramck's housing stock. The majority of houses in Hamtramck were built between 1915 and 1930 and were basic, if not primitive. Further, the neighborhoods were a mix of heavy industry and houses often clustered side by side. That was not an issue with the earlier immigrants who were just glad to have a place to live, especially close to their job sites, so they didn't have to take a streetcar. The postwar generation wasn't that concerned with streetcars, as they had their own cars. But that led to another problem: parking. With houses on lots thirty feet wide in Hamtramck and multifamily houses located side by like rows of dominoes, where do you fit in the cars? Answer: wherever you can. Hamtramck alone didn't prompt the growth of the suburbs; conditions in Detroit had more to do with that. In any case, communities like Warren, just north of Detroit, proved to be an irresistible lure. There were large lots with plenty of room for driveways, garages and expansive front and back lawns. Plus the infrastructure was much younger, so basements there didn't flood after a heavy rain like they tended to do (and still do) in older communities like Hamtramck.

This would lead to a steep population drop, especially between 1950 and 1960, when the population dipped from 45,355 to 34,137—and even much lower in later years.

The majority of houses in the city had undergone some degree of modernization through the years. By the late 1940s, almost all outdoor outhouses had been replaced by indoor toilets, although a few outhouses remained in the city until 1950. Coal- and wood-burning stoves had been replaced with gas models. Water heaters became common, and oil-burning furnaces replaced coal. There was no need to heat water on the stove anymore, and gas stoves with ovens made cooking much easier. Rooms in the houses were (and still are) fairly small, and many featured French doors between the living room and dining room. These could be closed during the winter so that only essential living space was fully heated to save on costs.

It wasn't luxury living, but there was a certain coziness about the spaces that made living there comfortable and comforting. By this time, almost all had radios, usually standup models that were pieces of furniture. In just a few years, television sets would be added to the roomscape. But in this time, reading and playing games were popular. And an advantage of radio is that you could do something else while listening. For example, many women crocheted and knitted as they listened to the radio.

But these houses lacked the conveniences of the modern houses being built in the suburbs. In Hamtramck, however, the housing market had been virtually devastated by the war. A report released in October 1945 by Investors Syndicate was stunning. In the three years of the war, home building in Hamtramck decreased by 99.1 percent compared to the three years prior to the war. That wasn't too surprising, considering the constraints on construction caused by the war. But some prewar figures were even more startling—only 423 of the city's 11,666 dwellings had been built since 1930.

"Volume of new home construction in Hamtramck during the combined three war years, 1942-43-44, provided for only 12 people against 1,380 provided for in the three pre-war years of 1939-40-41," said D.E. Ryan, vice president of Investors Syndicate.

"Valuation of new homes built during the combined three war years totaled $3,850 against the combined three-year pre-war aggregate of $1,193,011." He pointed out that no new homes had been built in the city in 1944. And in 1943, new dwelling units were made for a scant four people.

Ryan managed to put a positive spin on the numbers by noting, "A promising demand for new homes and considerable remodeling in your city is indicated."

And indeed, a wide-scale renovation was carried out in the city in the 1950s, although by then many people were leaving Hamtramck for the suburbs.

SURVIVAL
under
Atomic Attack

HAMTRAMCK OFFICE OF CIVIL DEFENSE
2361 Hewitt Avenue — TR. 4-2177

With the start of the Cold War following the end of World War II, the threat of nuclear attacks rose, even as the government attempted to downplay the potential devastation.

But that was still in the future, and with the return of the veterans in late 1945, a sense of vitality coursed through the city like the heavy traffic on Jos. Campau. By Christmas, stores were filling with merchandise. Rationing ended in August, and restaurants were able to serve up a wider variety of food. Even so, Three Star Steakhouse had to close for a while because of a shortage of ribs, which was its specialty. Dr. Goldberg's ads in the newspapers now promoted that his eye care was important because "Office workers need good vision." Earlier ads noted it was "soldiers" not "office workers" who needed to see well.

But an especially telling subtle shift was evident in, of all things, an ad for a child's wagon—the Atomic Koastmaster. It was advertised as "the newest idea in postwar wagons for children." Prior to World War II, the word *atomic* was pretty much reserved for scientific research. Now, it indicated power. Terrible power. The world had gone through a fundamental change as the atom had been released to be a weapon of war. And once released, it would never be eliminated, as we see even today. In the wake of World War II, the mystique of the atomic bomb would reach the level of a child's toy, although its vast power would only increase.

But the threat of the atomic bomb did not have worldwide reach at this point, as only the United States had the weapon. And this was a time of good feelings. The annual Goodfellows drive to raise money to buy Christmas gifts for needy children and the sons and daughters of men still in the service raised a record $8,045.45.

The people of Hamtramck closed out 1945 with the most joyous Christmas they had had in five years.

"This Christmas will be a merry and happy one for all the world is at peace again," wrote Cecilia Giza in *The Citizen* on December 21, 1945. "The people of Hamtramck, like people all over the world, are thankful for the war's end. Christmas Day will find the city's churches overcrowded. Crowds will throng to the churches with prayers for an everlasting peace. Mothers, wives and sweethearts will thank God for the safe return of their loved ones, while those of the dead will pray that their fighting boy's body may rest in peace."

Amen.

Experience It

Visit the memorial honoring the soldiers from Hamtramck who lost their lives in World War II, Korea and Vietnam. It also houses the grave of Colonel John Francis Hamtramck. Check out Dave Stober's name in the tile at the entrance of the store at 10012 Jos. Campau, just north of Yemans Street.

In the News

Hamtramck Sets New Tin Record

Hamtramck housewives helped establish a new tin can collection record Monday when they turned in 52,000 pounds of the prepared containers. Anthony G. Grodeski, chairman of the Hamtramck Salvage Board, said that the total is 14,000 pounds greater than the amount turned in during the drive held about two months ago.

—The Citizen, *March 2*

Rat Killing, Street Cleaning Urged by Ladislaus Students

The senior students of the St. Ladislaus School proved Tuesday that they had an extensive knowledge of city government....At the evening council meetings the students (proposed) several resolutions which would benefit the city, such as establishment of a new library and veteran's building, extermination of rats and cleaning up of streets.

—The Citizen, *May 25*

Week's Casualties Show One Killed, Two Wounded

Greater Hamtramck's shortest casualty list since the "all out" war began was issued this week by the War and Navy departments. One man was killed, two were wounded and one was freed. Of the four, three are Hamtramckans and the fourth is a North Detroiter.

—The Citizen, *July 6*

Father of 17 Injured in Furnace Explosion

The steam furnace of the service station at 12045 Jos. Campau exploded at about 11:45 a.m. last Friday. The door of the furnace was thrown across the street to the Bowery Café, where Julius Gonzales, Bowery day manager, was injured. Gonzales is the father of 17 children, ranging from 19 months to 22 years.

—The Citizen, *November 23*

7

1959

Clang... clang... clang...
        The sound echoed off the houses nearby with the rhythmic pace
        of footsteps.

Gary listened as he lay in bed. Despite its metallic beat, it was soothing, comforting. The pounding was steady and unending. It sounded like a heartbeat, and in a way, it was. Only the muscle that powered it was made of steel, and it didn't pump blood—it forged steel into the shape of auto parts. The big presses were active day and night at the Chevrolet Gear & Axle plant on St. Aubin Street and beyond, at the far western edge of Hamtramck. It was the little cousin of the big Dodge Main factory on the south side of the city.

But Gary didn't think of it that way. It was just another factory in town just like any of the others, only bigger. The main difference with the Chevy plant is that it had always been a part of his twelve-year-old life. And its eternal thumping was perfectly normal to him. It helped him sleep. The steady beat was oddly comforting and lulled him to oblivion. He needed the help this night. It was the end of Thursday, and while there was nothing special about this particular Thursday night, it did usher in Friday. And Friday was special. It was the close of the week, the last day of school before the weekend, and he just had to get through it to find the freedom the weekend brought.

Many thoughts floated through his mind as he lay in bed. There was so much in store. It was late September, so there was still plenty of time to play outside before the winter set in. Winter offered its own opportunities for having fun, but he preferred warm weather activities, like riding his bike. He especially liked to swerve around the curving bush-lined pathway that wound past the front of Hamtramck High School, just down from where he lived on Wyandotte Street. It got scarier and more exciting the faster you went, and so what if you took a spill and shredded your elbow every so often? No one ever seemed to get really hurt, even though no one wore helmets or elbow and knee guards at that time.

Then there was baseball. No, not at Veterans Memorial Park. That was for the big guys and rec department leagues. Gary and his friends played "home run or nothing" in the parking lot of the little old factory at the end of the block. There were no bases. You either hit a home run over the parking lot fence, usually slamming the ball off the aluminum siding of the house across the alley, or you were out. Amazingly, the people who owned the house didn't complain. Well, hardly ever complained, but the players used a hollow plastic ball and bat so no real damage was done. And they didn't hit that many homers anyway.

The curving path bordered by bushes around the Hewitt Street entrance of Hamtramck High School made a great bicycle racetrack for kids.

After bike riding, the pals might race their plastic model cars down "tar hill." That was a ramp-like structure (no one was sure what it was) that seemed like a mountain, although it probably was no more than fifteen feet high. Yet that was high enough to send the miniature cars racing down to the street level. The winner got nothing but satisfaction.

What if it rained? There were things to do indoors, like watching TV. There were ancient *Popeye* cartoons on Saturday and Sunday mornings, and Gary had developed his own list of favorite evening TV shows like *77 Sunset Strip* and *Twilight Zone* on Friday, *Leave It to Beaver* and *Have Gun, Will Travel* on Saturday and *Maverick* and especially *The Lawman* (the sheriff with the white stripe running through his hair) on Sunday.

Too much to think about. Gary couldn't sleep. He got up and went to the window, which was open. It was still warm outside, and he didn't have a window fan, so it was even hotter in his bedroom. It wasn't late, only about ten o'clock, but most everyone was home. Both sides of the street were lined with parked cars, and the old streetlight sent down a ring of light on the cars in front of the house next door. Over to the right he could see the brightness emanating from the Chevy factory, and of course, he could hear the clanging even more clearly. There was a sudden loud hiss that caused him to look toward the back of the factory site. He had heard it often before. The hissing was some sort of exhaust escaping into the sky. The plant did this often at night when you could hear what was being released into the air if you lived nearby, but you couldn't see it. Everyone just ignored it in those more innocent days when environment meant your home, not so much the world around you.

As abruptly as it started, it stopped, and Gary looked up, over the houses across the narrow street. He could pick out a fair number of stars in the night sky. At least the level of light pollution wasn't too bad yet. It would grow much worse in the years ahead. But Gary didn't know about that, and even if he did, he wouldn't have cared. His problems were more earthly, like how he hated school. And thinking of that, he realized that he had better get back in bed or he would never be able to crawl out of it in the morning.

He lay down, and while the clanging and lights outside might have seemed overwhelming, they were just parts of the portrait of his world. A part of him.

In the morning, his mom woke him at 7:00 a.m., and it was awful. But it was to be expected. Gary hated school. It was boring. It didn't interest him. It was confining, and each weekday began by attending Mass. Gary went to St. Florian Catholic School, which was only a few blocks from his

Going to a Catholic school meant going to Mass six days a week. The lower church at St. Florian was where the schoolkids went Monday through Friday.

house, so he could walk there even in the worst weather because they never, ever canceled a class because of bad weather even when the sky was falling in sheets of rain or avalanches of snowflakes. Nevertheless, each morning he dragged himself out of bed—or his mom did—and he got washed and dressed, gathered his books and trudged off into the elements, no matter what they were. Maybe he had done his homework the night before, maybe he hadn't.

Not even the fierceness of the Felician Sisters who lorded over the classrooms struck fear into him, or if they did, it usually didn't last for long. If he had learned anything in school, it was how to keep a low profile. And as much as he suffered through the seemingly endless hours in class, he did learn enough to get by, although his parents were already concerned about the twelve-year-old's future.

St. Florian wasn't a particularly large school. It was built on the corner of Florian and Brombach Streets in 1909 as a combined church-school building. That design was common in immigrant neighborhoods in those days. Most of the immigrants who came to Hamtramck in the second decade of the twentieth century were Polish, and most Poles were Catholic, so it was natural for them to gravitate to St. Florian. The building quickly became too small for its original use, and the church was moved out in 1914 when the basement church was built next door. That served as the foundation of the massive Gothic structure that was to be built in the mid-1920s. The original building was converted completely into a grade school, and a new front was added, with space in the basement—even the attic was divided into classrooms. Every inch was used, and by 1923 the building housed about 2,300 students. It was stupendously crowded. Lessons were straightforward, with an emphasis on the basics—reading, writing, 'rithmetic—and religion. This was Catholicism in its purest form. You were given the word of the Lord, and you listened. Don't ask questions. The nuns took a militant approach to teaching. Step out of line and you risked getting whacked with a yardstick.

It wasn't all drudgery. Every Friday afternoon, a music hour was broadcast over the PA system, and once a month, a movie was shown in the basement hall. Of course, there was only one projector, so about every ten minutes the movie was stopped while the reel of film was changed. And more than once a rolling reel of unraveling film was chased down the aisle by the kid running the projector who had dropped it.

But for Gary, more than anything, it was boring. Too often he watched the hands of the clock on the classroom wall crawl around the dial. And much of his time was spent staring out the window at the massive church building next door. Even at his young age, he was impressed. The structure was designed by architect Ralph Adams Cram (Gary didn't know that), who was famous in his time for his Gothic church designs across America. St. Florian was built between 1926 and 1928 in a modified English Gothic style. The original basement church was built to temporarily accommodate the growing number of parishioners. It would serve until the parishioners could gather up enough money to build a proper church. This was so important to them that many mortgaged their own houses to pay for the big structure. But even after that was done, the basement church was where the kids started each school day at Mass. The upstairs area was reserved for adults and for Sundays when everyone went to Mass.

If Gary was lucky, the nuns didn't call on him for anything throughout the day. If they did, he might know the answer to what they asked, or he might not. If he didn't know the answer, he might luck out, like the time he managed to read from the open textbook on his desk and recite the words of the answer to the question he had been asked. Even he was impressed with that one.

Alleys were never good places to play, but they had a certain charm for the kids—especially kids who were fond of hunting rats. Secure garbage cans significantly cut the rat population in later years.

And so it went, day after day, grade after grade. And despite his worst efforts, knowledge would seep into his brain. Eventually, he would go on to college, but that was too far ahead for him to imagine at this time in his life. What he could imagine was what was going to happen when the bell finally rang to signal the end of the school day—and the beginning of the part of the part of the day that mattered most.

And it rang. It was done. School was over for the week, and Friday had begun in earnest. Forget the homework. Never mind that Monday was just a few days away. What mattered was that it was Friday. And it came in with a built-in schedule of fun. He'd walk home from school, cutting through the alley between Wyandotte and Geimer Streets, past the unbroken line of barns that lined the alley, turning it into an urban canyon where, on occasion, he and his friend would hunt rats by placing bait at the foot of the wall, climbing up on the roof and dropping bricks on the unsuspecting rodents as they came out to grab the food below. Not particularly sporting, but hey, they were rats. Most days, though, he just used the alley as a back road to get to and from home. Almost all of the old barns were made of wood, and many had bowed roofs that appeared to be collapsing. The city had just started a program to have the barns torn down to give the city a cleaner, more modern look, but that happened slowly and sporadically.

Mom would be cleaning the house as Gary got home. She did that every Thursday and Friday. Thursday she cleaned the upstairs; Friday she did the downstairs. Everything was cleaned. The furniture was polished, and she even washed and waxed all the floors. Gary would help, sometimes, mainly polishing the furniture. Dad worked the afternoon shift, so he wouldn't be home until much later. At dinnertime, the evening fun would begin. Mom would take Gary and his little sister, Kate, out for a walk to Jos. Campau Avenue, over to Nichol's restaurant near Holbrook Avenue. It was a small, somewhat cramped place that had great service and terrific food, particularly the salmon patties. Remember, this was Friday, and for Catholics, that meant no meat to eat.

After dinner, it was time to shop. Jos. Campau was a carnival of stores. It had been the main street of Hamtramck since at least the 1880s, and it had grown to be a major shopping area. In fact, by the 1950s Jos. Campau

In a way, Jos. Campau Avenue was a street of dreams. It was a wonderland of stores of all types. It reached its peak in the 1950s.

was the second-most popular shopping district in southeast Michigan. Only downtown Detroit did more business than the stores on Jos. Campau. The whole length in Hamtramck ran barely more than a mile and a half, but it was the quarter-mile section that ran through the center of town where most of the action was. That stretch was considerably narrower than the portions on the north and south, giving it a more intense feel of activity. A huge number of projecting business signs closed it in even further. Along the strip, you could find everything: clothing, shoes, jewelry, fabrics, furniture, hardware, tools, food and drinks, as the strip boasted a fair number of bars mixed in with everything else. Mom worked for a time at Brawer's, a "dime store" that featured a wide variety of things. At one time, it even housed a mynah bird that spoke Polish and swore at customers (so it had to be put in a back room periodically until it lost that skill). The quality of the merchandise was questionable, but not the price. It was cheap in every sense of the word. But Brawer's was just south of the main shopping area, so it didn't always make the Friday shopping expedition. But the three big department stores—Neisner's, Grant's and Kresge's—all did. And it would be at one of these that Gary would find a treasure, usually a plastic model airplane or car that could be bought for all of twenty-nine cents. Kate would get her own toy, and their mom would get whatever she wanted.

If something more substantial was required, the crew would go to Federal's department store. This three-story emporium was for heavy-duty shopping. Often things would cost so much that Mom would have to put the item on layaway. The store would hold it in reserve until she paid off the full amount at a few dollars a week. Leaving the store, they cut back across the street to Jeanette's Book Store to buy a birthday card for someone. The store seemed incredibly tight, even for a kid. The counters loomed up along both sides of the center aisle, and merchandise was jammed together. The staff could have used a lesson on customer relations, as it seemed like they couldn't wait for you to leave. But you would find what you wanted there. Then there might be a stop at Sweetland's to pick up some candy or, better yet, get some ice cream. Other stops would depend on what was on the shopping list. Mom could get shoes at Shapiro's, a dress at Day's Fashions, a new watch at Max's jewelry store and just about anything else she could possibly need was somewhere on Jos. Campau.

By the time they were heading back home, it was getting dark, but there were still plenty of people walking on the sidewalks or riding bikes or trying to make their way down Jos. Campau through a heavy stream of traffic. As they passed the tightly grouped houses, most only five feet apart, some of the folks sitting on the porches would wave and say hello. This was a time before

Jeanette's Book Store was tiny yet packed with books, greeting cards and more.

most homes had air conditioning, and there no computers with their games to draw the kids indoors. But there was TV. By the late '50s, almost everyone had a TV, and there was a fairly extensive assortment of shows to watch. Gary switched on the TV set but really didn't pay attention to what was on. He wanted to check out the plastic model airplane he had just gotten. Kate got a new doll, but she was so tired after the long walk that she was more interested in just sitting for a while and soon was asleep in her chair.

Cunningham's Drug Stores anchored the north and south ends of Jos. Campau where it narrowed between Caniff and Holbrook Streets. They were favorites on the strip.

At 9:00 p.m., Gary switched on *77 Sunset Strip*, which he liked since it was likely that a bad guy would get beaten up. But by the time the fateful fight occurred, Gary was too tired to care, so he went to bed. He had wanted to stay up until Dad got home from work but just couldn't make it. All in all, it had been a pretty good day, he thought, as he drifted off.

Saturday morning began with a bang. Actually, three bangs. Mom and Dad already were up and downstairs. She was calling everyone down for breakfast with the aid of a broomstick that she used to pound on the ceiling, or floor, depending on which side of the broom you were on. In any case, it worked, and Gary fell out of bed, got dressed and stumbled downstairs. Talk at the breakfast table centered on Mom and Dad and Dad's job. He worked at the Dodge Main factory and was glad to be back at the job. He had been off for six weeks while the factory switched over to producing the 1960 models, including the new Dodge Valiant and Dart. This was a big deal for the plant, as thousands of employees had been laid off temporarily while 1.3 million square feet of the Dodge plant total of 5 million square feet was being redone to accommodate production of the Valiant alone. The new models required modern production processes, including greater welding capacity to handle the heavier gauge steel being used in the new models. And a new painting process was being introduced.

Anything that affected the Dodge Main factory was important to Hamtramck because it was the biggest taxpayer by far in the city. And more than once it paid its taxes early to bail the city out of a cash shortage that it experienced periodically. Paradoxically, even as it came to Hamtramck's rescue financially, Chrysler was battling the city for a $871,748.10 tax refund, saying its property tax assessment was too high. Such disagreements were not unusual, however, and did no damage to the city and company's relationship. But this year, there were fears that Chrysler was considering closing the factory. That was heightened when C. Pat Quinn, president of the Dodge Local 3 employees' union, advised workers to "leave Detroit" because the plant was closing and operations would be transferred to the Chrysler plant on Jefferson Avenue in Detroit. Quinn made the statement to nearly four thousand Chrysler employees who had gathered at Keyworth Stadium on a Sunday in July. Dodge Main general management responded with a statement: "Throughout Dodge's forty-five-year history we have found Hamtramck a friendly, convenient and pleasant community in which to work….We expect to be here for some time and hope that other businesses will join us." The "other businesses" reference was in connection with the city's drive at the time to bring more companies into Hamtramck.

Restarting operations at Dodge Main with two new models was itself a statement that Dodge Main's future in Hamtramck was secure. And it would be for another two decades.

The other big topic of the breakfast discussion was the championship Little League team. The Hamtramck team had just won the World Championship, decimating the California team, 12–0. The team was powered by Art "Pinky" Deras, who has since been dubbed as the finest Little League player of all time. Deras tossed seven consecutive tournament shutouts, leading to the championship. "Deras rates in a class by himself. I've never seen a boy of his age who could match him," said Dr. Creighton Hale, who worked for the Little League to evaluate players.

The win brought joy to all of Hamtramck and was capped by the announcement that the boys would appear on *The Lawrence Welk Show*, which just so happened to be sponsored by the Chrysler Corp. Dodge Division. This might have mattered more to Gary if he played Little League ball, but he preferred playing in the factory lot down the street. But there is no denying that it was big news.

After breakfast, Gary was ready to head outside to enjoy the sunshine. He wasn't sure what he was going to do. He could meet up with some friends and go bike riding. They might go over to the old Acme Paint plant

The Hamtramck Little League team achieved international fame when they won the World Championship in 1959. The team's success was the hottest news around Hamtramck in the summer of that year.

at the end of St. Aubin Street and play in the abandoned Quonset huts there. They were spooky. Or he might ride over to Hamtramck High School just for fun. If he was really bored, he might go and play with the girls down the street, but they usually wanted to play school. Gary could not understand why they wanted to pretend to be in school when they were there for real all week. In any case, it didn't matter. Mom had other plans for him. "I want you to go over to the Kucway's market and buy a pound of bacon. Here's fifty cents," she said and handed him two quarters. "Bring back the change." Bacon then was twenty-nine cents a pound. Kucway's market was one of the myriad markets that stood almost on every second corner. It was across from Jean's store on Faber and Lumpkin Streets, just a few blocks from Gary's house. He could have ridden his bike there but decided to walk. It gave him a chance to take a look around. He was still awfully young but was becoming more aware of the world around him. He noticed that the street he walked down had changed in recent years. It took a while, but he realized that the trees weren't the same. There were fewer of them than there had been just a short while ago. They used to form a big leafy roof arching over the street, kind of like the ceiling of St. Florian Church. Now he could see only sky with some shorter trees lining the streets. He had seen people cutting trees down on some blocks but did not know why. But he was right. The trees were gone, and more were doomed. Dutch elm disease was spreading across the United States, killing the trees. In the early 1950s, Hamtramck had more than three thousand elm trees. In 1955, several cases of the disease were detected by the city. The trees were cut down, and it looked as though the threat had been checked. It wasn't. More cases cropped up, and eventually, nearly all the elm trees were cut down or died. Their loss dramatically changed the appearance of Hamtramck. The city lost the rural tint it had had despite the factories and commercial buildings. It took on a harsher appearance. Where there had been cool shadows now was hot pavement baked in the glare of the sun.

The houses were also changing. Wooden stairs and porches were being replaced by brick and stone. The wooden slat sides of the houses were being covered by aluminum siding, and that strange substance called Mural stone, a type of brick, was being attached to houses all over. It was neater, more modern, yet sterile. It seemed more suited to new suburban houses than the older Hamtramck structures that had their own classic character.

Gary passed by a house surrounded by a low fence with two signs side by side. He had seen them before and thought them very curious. One said, "Elect Albert J. Zak Mayor," the other, "Promote Henry R. Kozak Mayor." What's that all about? he thought. They were leftovers from the previous fall's election, which pitted incumbent mayor Al Zak against challenger Henry Kozak in what had been a contentious race. It was the "Zak" "Kozak" that caught Gary's attention. It almost sounded like the same name but wasn't. Zak, who served in the 1950s to early 1960s and then came back to serve again as mayor in the early 1970s, was probably Hamtramck's most popular mayor. He presided over the city in what is often considered its golden age. It was a time that Hamtramckans view as the city's greatest era of prosperity, when it was a spotlessly clean, mythically peaceful place characterized by peace and love. Some of that was true. Most of it wasn't. "City Financial Outlook Bleak" was the banner headline on the front page of *The Citizen* newspaper on June 11, 1959.

"Hamtramck's municipal financial outlook was at its lowest point this week when the machinery started grinding away on the Chrysler Corporation's appeal for a 75% tax cut on its Hamtramck properties," the story read. "To make matters even bluer, the City's 400 some workers went without their paychecks yesterday for the first time in years."

Zak? Kozak? Despite the similarity of the names, these were two fierce political rivals. But Zak was the winner.

Perhaps the story painted too bleak of a picture, but it was true that a financial cancer was eating away at the city's health. An overly generous pension system, declining population, aging infrastructure and years of questionable management and even some outright corruption were gradually catching up with the town. While the Jos. Campau shopping district remained strong, there were already serious fears among the store owners that the growing threat of the new suburban shopping malls was going to undermine their businesses. They were right to worry. The financial collapse wouldn't happen until the early 1970s, when the city's failing finances were taken over by the state, but the signs of pending trouble were already showing in the 1950s. Most people who look at Hamtramck today lament the loss of those golden days without ever realizing that they weren't quite as golden as they remember. Mayor Zak seemed to understand the seriousness of the situation but wasn't able to do much about it. No one wanted to cut anything, including the four hundred some employees who worked for the city at that time. As for Gary, he was left to wrestle with the Zak-Kozak mystery until his dad explained it to him.

Meanwhile, he bought the bacon.

Gary spent the rest of the day with his best friend, Ben, riding bikes and playing games. Later, he built his plastic model plane. He also made plastic model cars, which his mom put on display in the upstairs hallway. He was very proud of them and appreciated the attention his mom gave to them. He slept well that night.

Sunday morning was a repeat of Saturday, beginning with the same banging on the ceiling/floor. Then breakfast—eggs (with bacon)—but then it was off to church for noon Mass. Frankly, that was an exercise in daydreaming. No matter how much he tried and how hard he worried that he was doomed to eternity in Hell, he just couldn't concentrate on what was going on. Maybe it was a case of overkill. Going to church six days a week would challenge the faith of any kid. And he never forgot the image of the young girl in the pew in front of him who fainted during an early morning Mass and bounced like a pinball machine ball as she fell forward, hitting her head, then backward to the seat, then sideways and finally forward again on the floor. She survived.

Plus, the pews were made of hard wood that made sitting uncomfortable.

After church, though, the family was in for a real treat. They got into their Dodge and headed for Kensington Metropark for a daylong picnic. His dad loved that state park, about thirty-five miles northwest of Hamtramck, near Milford, Michigan. It was a great break from the city. It was everything the city wasn't, filled with raw nature not tamed by asphalt, concrete and steel. Kent Lake adjoined the park and had a fine beach that was clean and comfortable except for the one time Gary stepped on a bee. That left

Kids loved pizza in 1959 as much as they do today. These hungry adventurers were taking part in a city-sponsored Recreation Department trip.

a lasting impression. Mom packed a cooler with sandwiches enough for everyone, which somehow tasted even better in the open air. The journey home in the late afternoon was made longer because Dad liked to take the route "around the lakes," meaning the variety of lakes dotting the rural areas away from metro Detroit. He would stay off the main roads and drive on the meandering roads that passed by many lakes. By the time they got home, everyone was exhausted but happy.

Gary managed to watch *The Lawman* and even *The Rebel* before he had had enough for the day. In the settling darkness, he again stood by the open window of his bedroom. This time, he could hear the horn of a distant train. The tracks ran through the Chevy plant. The distance softened the train's wail into a gentle, soothing call. He didn't like the thought of having to get up tomorrow and go back to school. But he felt comfortable, as if everything was right with him and the world.

He went to bed.

EXPERIENCE IT

Go to the intersection of Brombach and Poland Streets and one block south to Florian Street. This area has been virtually unchanged since 1959. St. Florian School, built in 1909 and also still unchanged, is operating, although now as a charter school.

In the News

Chrysler Will Keep Conant Stamping Division in City

Eighteen hundred employees at the Conant Stamping Division of the Chrysler Corporation received the glad news today that operations of the plant will remain in Hamtramck. The corporation revealed that it had cancelled previously announced plans to transfer operations from the local factory at 8021 Conant to other plants in Detroit and Ohio.

—The Citizen, February 19

Free Text Books and Lunches Eliminated by School Board

While Hamtramck's school children slept Monday night, the School Board voted away, one by one, virtually every advantage they had over their Detroit counterparts. (Due to budget cuts) there will be no dental clinic, no free lunches for Pulaski School crippled children, no classroom magazines, fewer new texts and library books.

—The Citizen, April 16

Basements Flood after New Relief Sewer Opened

Elimination of flood conditions, which occurred at every heavy rain, at the Conant Avenue viaduct, was a boon to motorists but it has raised havoc in basements of nearby homes, the City Council was told by a delegation of residents Tuesday.

—The Citizen, August 27

Banquet Tuesday Night Honoring Little Leaguers

"The big night—Tuesday, Oct. 27—that has been set aside by the community to honor its World Championship Little Leaguers is less than a week away," commented National Little League President Edward Kopek.

—The Citizen, October 22

8

1968

The beat of the DRUM sounded for the first time in May 1968, and its listeners followed in step.

DRUM was the Dodge Revolutionary Union Movement, which was created by a group of Black workers at the Dodge Main factory who were angry and frustrated with the United Auto Workers, their official union. They felt their concerns were being ignored despite the fact that 70 percent of the workers at the plant were Black. That this happened then is not surprising. In ways, 1968 was a pivotal year for the entire nation. Through the 1960s, emphasis on racial equality was gaining momentum. The Civil Rights Act of 1964 and Voting Rights Act of 1965 brought a sharper focus on discrimination and stirred movements to seek equality for all. And like a wave, the force gathered momentum as calls for justice evolved into demands.

This wasn't embraced by all, and through the 1960s, a series of riots occurred in cities across the nation, including Detroit in July 1967.

Yet even as Detroit burned, Hamtramck was calm. In a way, that is symbolic of the Black/White relations in Hamtramck. In one sense, the city has been a remarkably welcoming community in eras when segregation was the norm. Yet examples of blatant racism are not uncommon. Of course, nothing is ever simple in Hamtramck, and the contradictory character was simply the way things were. But it would be wrong to assume that the Black residents of Hamtramck didn't recognize racism and stand up to it with a determination that was powerful and unrelenting.

drum

VOL. 2 NO. 16 REVOLUTIONARY UNION MOVEMENT

LILY WHITE—SUPER RIGHT

LILY WHITE, SUPER RIGHT INJUST_
ICE against BLACKS
   Prejudice, racism, favori-
tism, chaos and confusion; all
of the things that Chrysler is
against was supported by them
Thursday, May 8, 1969. There
was a hillbilly, razor back who
referred to a black brother as
a "nigger". This was said to
Brother John who works as an
inspector in dept. 3200, 6th
floor, big line. Bro. John got
the steward and the tom ass labor relations man, Young, on
the case. After the wet back
Chuck saw that Bro John was going to take action he then apo-
logized. He said he was sorry
in front of the house nigger
and the UAW toms. This was enough for management: the labor
relations house nigger Young,
said that there was nothing,
that he could do after the hill
-billy had said he was sorry.
Young said that Bro John should
be a big man because this was
something that he would have to

live with in this society !
This hillbilly disrespected all
black men's manhood and showed
no respect for Bro John as a
man but as a nigger (which is
nothing; a nigger is something
neutral which cannot function,
under its own power; a nigger
has no brains, the white man
thinks for him completely) .
This is discrimination and prejudice coming from the hillbilly. And Chrysler stood by and
allowed this to happen.
8   How long are we as black
men going to allow this to happen? We must take a stand a-
gainst this type of thing .
This type of racism is all over
this plant, all departments.
Chrysler knows it and yet it is
happening because 95% of all
foreman are hillbilly slavedri-
vers. Hillbilly George Harpers
knows this type of thing happen
and does nothing about it and
this is one of the reasons it
is still happening. The other
reason is that we, as black men

DRUM was the publication of the Dodge Revolutionary Union Movement, which
was started by a group of Black United Auto Workers who were dissatisfied with the
representation they were getting with the UAW.

   Black people have lived in Hamtramck since its township days. The 1827
Census lists seven Black residents. But it really wasn't until the late 1910s
that Black residents began to receive more attention because they were
building political power. Essentially, they could not be ignored, because

at that time, the longtime German residents and the newly arriving Polish immigrants were in a struggle over who would have political control over the then Village of Hamtramck. Records and facts of this period are sketchy, but the Polish politicians appealed to the Black residents and won their support in the movement to incorporate Hamtramck as a city in 1922. The Poles' efforts were successful, and the population voted in favor of incorporation. But even before that took place, Black status was growing in town. Ordine Toliver, one of Hamtramck's most prominent Black residents, served on the last village council in 1921. Toliver later held a variety of positions in city government. He also operated a music studio where he taught students, mostly White kids.

And he wasn't the only Black Hamtramckan to find success in the mostly White town. Dr. James Henderson, a Black physician, was named to the first city council when it was formed in 1922. He also went on to serve the city in other capacities, including as city physician.

There are other remarkable examples of racial acceptance in a period when racism was common throughout America. During the 1920s, the

Ordine Toliver examines the voter rolls with Mayor Al Zak. Toliver was a Black man who rose to high office in Hamtramck in a time when Black people were held back from positions of stature. He was highly regarded by Black and White citizens alike.

139

Hamtramck has traditionally been a welcoming city, where for the most part people of all races and nationalities and religions have lived together in harmony.

Hamtramck Police Department was fully integrated, and there were even Black police detectives on the force through the years. The Hamtramck Public Schools also were fully integrated by the 1920s. And it was genuine integration. Kids were not segregated in the classrooms, and Black and White boys and girls played together on the numerous school sports teams.

But perhaps the most meaningful example is that as early as the 1920s, some Black and White residents lived in separate flats in the same multifamily houses. White kids often had Black friends, and they would all go on day trips together sponsored by the Hamtramck Recreation Department.

No studies were done on how this unusual degree of togetherness came about, but some have speculated that the poor Polish immigrants, who were almost at the bottom of the social ladder, felt a kinship with Black people, who were at the bottom. They shared misery, and that allowed them to sympathize and relate with each other.

It sounds idyllic, but of course the story was much more complicated than that. While there were great examples of cooperation and togetherness, there were also incidents of raw racism. But one thing that is not disputable is that the Black community was organized and willing to fight for justice. Early on, they took a stand that they would be heard, and if those in charge wouldn't listen, they would speak up louder.

The Black community got a sense of strength with Ordine Toliver and Dr. Henderson holding council seats, even if only for a relatively brief time. But they demonstrated that the Black community did have a place at the center of power. In 1924, the Poles took virtually complete political control of the city. For the next seventy years or so, virtually every person elected to public office in Hamtramck would be Polish or of Polish descent. But the Black community exercised a degree of power of their own. In the 1920s and 1930s, they applied pressure on the mayor and other officials, whoever they might be, to appoint Black leaders to important positions.

In April 1936, the Black community threw its support behind incumbent city clerk Frank Matulewicz, who was seeking reelection. Matulewicz had appointed Ordine Toliver as assistant city clerk. Matulewicz won, defeating his opponent by a two-to-one margin. That guaranteed Toliver at least another two years in his post. The Black vote played a major role in that election. Incumbent mayor Rudolph Tenerowicz won reelection after campaigning hard for Black support, which he received. "I am grateful for the wonderful support that the colored people gave me in my campaigns....I will be a good mayor," Tenerowicz said when the results came in. Also winning with Black support was controversial candidate Mary Zuk. Long accused of being a communist (which she neither admitted nor denied), Zuk campaigned on a platform of "full social and political rights to the Negro citizens."

City Assessor Vincent Sadlowski was one of the first department heads appointed by Tenerowicz, and he named Eugene Butler, a Black man, as assistant city assessor.

In July 1936, Mayor Tenerowicz got a further pat from the Black community following an incident that turned racial. The police department came under fire by some residents when Black police officer Clifton Mobley was accused of using undue force in arresting a White man. But Police Chief William Berg and Public Safety Commissioner Richard Connell Jr. defended Mobley, saying he was acting in the line of duty and punishing him would show a disrespect for the law.

"The courageous action of Chief Berg and Commissioner Connell reflects favorable [sic] upon the administration of Mayor Tenerowicz. The mayor is also to be commended for his selection of such fine men to fill these important posts. Their fairness will always be remembered by the colored citizens of Hamtramck," LeRoy G. White wrote in the *Detroit Tribune* on July 4, 1936. That commendation would translate into votes at election time.

Was all of this a result of social justice, or was it political expediency? There is no way of knowing now for sure, but it likely was a mix of both. And it got Black people into positions that were unattainable in many other towns.

The Black community also scored a major political victory with the election of Charles Diggs to the state senate in November 1936. Diggs, who represented the Third District, which also included a part of Detroit, was the first Black Democrat to be elected to the state senate. He defeated three Black and two White candidates for the post. The progress of the Black community was aided by a network of churches and social organizations. Corinthian Baptist Church, St. Peter's AME, Quinn Chapel, First Institutional Baptist Church and others served not only as places of worship but also as community centers, which helped build bonds among the members and enhanced the sense of solidarity. While they would hold lectures on politics or serious social issues, they also engaged in community fun, like fashion shows held to raise money for charity.

The 1930s also saw the promotion of the Self Respect Campaign, which was instituted by the *Detroit Tribune*, a Black newspaper, which regularly devoted a section to the happenings in Hamtramck. As the name indicated, the organization was designed to help promote a sense of self-respect with the basic tenet that Black residents were just as worthy as White residents and entitled to the same rights and privileges. Councilwoman Mary Zuk, who supported the campaign, reinforced the concept that Blacks and Poles had a common base. She said, in the *Voice of the People* publication: "We believe that the poor Whites are traveling the same road as the Negro citizens and should unite with them to fight their common oppressors." Zuk wanted the Self Respect Campaign to become affiliated with her group, the People's League. LeRoy White, who worked for the *Detroit Tribune* and founded the Self Respect Campaign, seemed to take a step back, likely noting Zuk's communist connections. "We appreciate the offer of the People's League," he said, "but I am not in a position to accept the offer without the consent of the majority of the colored citizens." It's not clear if that ever came. In any case, the struggle went on relentlessly. While great progress was made in some areas, setbacks occurred in others. One of the worst events took place in August 1934 at the Quinn Chapel AME Church, which was located at the corner of Mackay and Holmes Streets. It was surrounded by White residents who objected to the Black church being in their midst. After several

HAMTRAMCK HOUSING COMMISSION
COL. HAMTRAMCK HOMES
12025 DEQUINDRE AVENUE
HAMTRAMCK 12, MICHIGAN

Race relations have been remarkably cordial in Hamtramck, but it hasn't been perfect. When the Col. Hamtramck Homes were built in the early 1940s, they were reserved for White residents only.

incidents of harassment—stones being thrown at church windows, White residents blocking the front stairs—a riot nearly broke out at the church. Eventually, the frustrated parishioners closed the building and moved to a site in Detroit. Yet this occurred only a few months after two White women were fired from their jobs at Winnie White's Confectionary on Jos. Campau Avenue for refusing to serve a Black customer.

That wasn't the only example of racial divide that characterized Hamtramck's race relations. While it was common in neighborhoods for Black and White residents to live side by side, and in some cases, in the same multifamily house, as noted earlier, the opening of the Col. Hamtramck Homes housing project in the early 1940s sparked perhaps the worst case of racial discrimination in the city's history, at least until that time. In 1939, the city proposed building the housing complex at the far northwest side of town next to the railroad tracks. It would include three hundred housing units that would feature "low rent" covering "heating, electricity, gas and water bills" and include "a gas range, refrigerator, automatic water heater." The city received a federal grant of $1,263,000 to construct the site. It was viewed as a welcome addition to the city, but when the units were built and it came time to rent them, the Hamtramck Housing Commission, under intense pressure from some groups in the city, including the Hamtramck Tax Payers Association, ruled that no Black persons would be allowed to live there. The argument used was that mixing Black and White tenants would promote friction. The Black community was outraged and almost immediately filed a lawsuit against the exclusionary policy. This led to a twelve-year court battle that rejected segregation and opened the units to all.

But even as the worst of the controversy played out, some White Hamtramckans took up the cause of disenfranchised Black people. Thomas Dombrowski, who had long connections to the local communists, spoke at a rally in 1942 in support of the Black community. So did George Kristalsky, another longtime communist who frequently ran for public office (but never won). But this wasn't about communism or capitalism. It was about justice. And in 1954, the courts agreed, and the homes were integrated.

In a way, this was a precursor of what was to come with the city's urban renewal program that devolved into a tragedy of historic proportions. Its roots traced to the 1940s, in the wake of World War II, when the whole nation was reevaluating its infrastructure. As early as 1940, the city did a survey of Hamtramck buildings and determined that about 25 percent of the nearly 12,000 units in Hamtramck were substandard. The Hamtramck Housing Commission noted in its annual report the "amazing fact" that 1,710 units still had outdoor toilets. Many more were rated as "substandard." This report was used as ammunition to convince the city to build the public housing that the Col. Hamtramck Homes would provide, and it worked. The housing project was built, although it prompted the long court case. It also promoted bad feelings between the Black and White residents. That persisted through the 1950s and 1960s, although it never reached a boiling point. Black and White residents lived side by side in many areas, but they still could not share seats at the snack bars in the department stores on Jos. Campau. They were segregated. But change was coming.

January 1968 arrived in Hamtramck on a note of promise. On January 9, the city received word from the federal government that a $1.2 million grant had been approved for Hamtramck to jump-start the Wyandotte Street area urban renewal project. This, which became known as the R-31 area, stretched from Jos. Campau Avenue and Holbrook Street at the east and north to Hewitt and Dubois Streets to the south and west. The ambitious project would cover the demolition of 125 buildings, including 23 commercial structures. That included the venerable Hamtramck High

School, which was built in 1915 and expanded over the following years. By this time, 49 buildings had already been demolished in the area. Among those targeted was a series of "flat tops," multifamily houses with flat roofs, which were decaying and substandard. They were occupied mainly by Black families on Wyandotte Street. The plan was to clear the entire site and build a new city hall, police station and fire station there.

This was an era of change, and almost no one raised voices of concern about the project. But at this point, there was little to lose. The whole project would be covered by federal funds so there would be no increase in local taxes. It all seemed innocent enough. Hamtramck never had a city hall. The old village hall also included the police and fire departments, and it was far too small from the day it opened in 1915 to serve the community adequately. As a result, city offices were scattered in locations around the town, which was inefficient and impractical. The school board agreed to sell the high school to the city with the stipulation that the site be used only for municipal purposes and not be sold to a housing developer.

By the 1950s, Hamtramck's housing stock was low, and there were many substandard houses, such as these "flat tops" on Alice Street. That prompted the city to begin a major urban renewal program.

While this was going on, other changes were occurring in the city. Father Peter Walkowiak, longtime pastor of St. Florian Parish, died and was replaced by a new pastor, Father Joseph Kubik, who promised to bring a new sense of energy to the aging parish. In February, the upcoming city primary election was shaping up to be the most boring in the city's history. Only 13,806 people were registered to vote, and only a handful of candidates had filed to run. Things got a little more lively just before the election when former mayor Al Zak filed to run against incumbent Joseph Grzecki Sr. Zak, who had been an especially popular mayor in the 1950s, would come close but came in second in the primary election, setting the stage for a heated general election.

In March, the city put out bids for a new city hall to be constructed on the urban renewal site. The design of the new building was sleek and modern. As this was taking place, Zak and Grzecki waged fierce campaigns, each claiming they would eliminate blight and clean and modernize the city. In the end, Grzecki prevailed in the general election, although this was hardly the finish for Zak, who would return to office in the early 1970s.

As Easter approached in early April, the city, and the whole nation, was stunned by the assassination of Dr. Martin Luther King Jr. Rioting broke out in some cities, but Hamtramck was quiet. This was despite the fact that the wounds of the 1967 insurrection in Detroit were still fresh and the whole area was on edge. Local police patrols were boosted, with officers working twelve-hour shifts starting Friday, the day after the assassination. Soon units of the Michigan National Guard were sent to reinforce the police. For a time, military trucks and Jeeps were parked at the St. Florian Education Center on Poland Street. An 8:00 p.m. curfew had been put into place, and there were few reports of violations. Basically, all was calm. At least on the surface.

In fact, the whole nation was in great turmoil. The Vietnam War was worsening, and anti-war rallies were increasing. Race relations were at a modern low. Many young people were rebelling against the norms of their parents, and it looked like American society was fraying. In one sense, it was a vibrant time. Jos. Campau Avenue was packed with shoppers. Dodge Main, Chevrolet Gear & Axle and the numerous smaller factories scattered all over the area were buzzing and sometimes roaring with energy and activity. There was a feeling of energy pulsating through the community. But in another sense, much of the energy was just what it seemed to be—noise. Hamtramck High School was symbolic of what the city was experiencing. It was a majestic building that once ranked among the finest schools in the nation. By 1968, the walls were crumbling, and the roof was leaking to such

Sites like this on the city's South End were unacceptable and needed to be cleared.

an extent that the educational North Central Association said that if repairs were not made at once the school would lose accreditation. At the same time, St. Francis Hospital was facing the same situation and was on the verge of closing. Neither of these cases came as a surprise to the city, which was one reason so much emphasis was placed on the urban renewal program and how it might revitalize the city.

But there was dissent growing about the program. Some residents of the R-31 Wyandotte Street area project objected to it, complaining that houses were being acquired and demolished without justification. While no one defended the removal of the old flattops on Wyandotte Street, which were clearly decrepit, others noted that seemingly fine homes were being acquired and destroyed. Were people using the program to sell their house to the government and taking the money to move to the suburbs? Considering the level of corruption seen so often through the years, it wasn't surprising that the urban renewal program came under fire.

This feeling wasn't limited to Hamtramck. In July 1969, Governor George Romney signed a new law to protect persons from losing their homes in urban renewal programs. "The right of people to be secure in their homes is a basic American precept," Romney said. "It follows that no government or public agency has the right to dislodge people from their homes without accepting a degree of responsibility for that action and for their future housing." The bill required "a feasible method of relocation of displaced families shall demonstrate that standard housing units are or will be available to displaced families and individuals at rent prices within their financial means." But that meant little except to the relatively small group of residents living in the R-31 area. And whatever noise they made was quickly lost in the uproar that occurred days later when residents received their tax bills, which included a 40 percent tax hike. The hike was due to a school millage approved by residents that turned out to be higher than they expected and increased pension costs for police and fire personnel. In spite of that noise, the city went forward with creating a master plan to revitalize the shopping district, the schools and city operations. Developed by the City Planning Association of Mishawaka, Indiana, the plan even recommended making Jos. Campau Avenue a one-way street so it would be more friendly to shoppers. Planning had never been a strong point of the city officials, and this plan, which made some excellent, if somewhat obvious suggestions like the school buildings need to be rebuilt, went nowhere. But other plans were being made. In September, Mayor Grzecki met with the U.S. Housing and Urban Development representatives on a proposal for a $20 million redevelopment project for the city.

That plan got a big boost in October when the city was awarded $3.8 million for the Wyandotte project. Later that month, the city received even more good news when the Chrysler Corporation denied (again) reports that it was going to close the Dodge Main plant and move operations to Troy, Michigan. Those rumors were sparked by an article that appeared in the *Michigan Chronicle* newspaper saying the company was concerned that members of DRUM—the Dodge Revolutionary Union Movement—were going to sabotage operations at the plant. Remember, DRUM was the labor movement started by Black Dodge employees who felt disenfranchised by the UAW.

"The activities of DRUM and the Black workers at Hamtramck have not affected any long-range planning. There hasn't been any sabotage in the plant, and we don't anticipate any," the company stated. Yet the fact that there was even a rumor of closing showed the strained racial tensions that had become common at that time.

In November, the urban renewal project picked up even more momentum when the city created a "field office" to oversee the purchase of properties

SOUTH END RENEWAL PROJECT

IN DYNAMIC
HAMTRAMCK

THE BIRTH PLACE & HOME TOWN OF

CHRYSLER
DODGE MAIN PLANT

25 ACRES ZONED FOR HEAVY MANUFACTURING

CONTAINING
IDEAL SITES FOR INUSTRIAL & COMMERCIAL
ENTERPRISES

LOCATED IN THE HEART OF THE AUTOMOBILE
INDUSTRY

▼

PREPARED UNDER THE DIRECTION OF:

ALBERT J. ZAK
MAYOR
MICHAEL J. MOZOLA
DIRECTOR OF URBAN RENEWAL

3201 ROOSEVELT AVE.
HAMTRAMCK 12, MICHIGAN
TRINITY 4-3884

SPONSORED BY THE UNITED STATES GOVERNMENT AND
THE CITY OF HAMTRAMCK FOR INDUSTRIAL REDEVELOPMENT

Several areas of the city were designated for renewal, including the industrial area around the Dodge Main factory. But it was the R-31 area centered on Wyandotte Street that prompted the most problems.

Mayor Joseph Grzecki Sr. digs into the urban renewal program at a groundbreaking ceremony.

in the R-31 Wyandotte Street area. The office was to negotiate prices with homeowners and proceed to carry out condemnations in circuit court with owners who refused to comply.

So the stage was set for disaster.

In late November, an organization called the South End Improvement Association filed a lawsuit against the city alleging the urban renewal plan did not include enough housing affordable to the Black residents who would be displaced by the project. Further, it was viewed that the project was being used as a way to get Black residents out of the city. Like a snowball rolling down a hill, this progressed into an avalanche. A key piece of evidence was an inflammatory tape recording made at one of the meetings of the field office in which the urban renewal director said the residents had to support the program or risk having Hamtramck turn into "another Mississippi." It wasn't direct, but the meaning was clear: support urban renewal, or the city will be taken over by Black people.

Ultimately, the city would be found guilty of "Negro removal" and ordered to provide housing for the displaced. But that is equivalent to saying the Encyclopedia Britannica is a bunch of books about things. The reality was a legal case that has stretched on for more than fifty years and is only now concluding as this is being written. Suffice it to say the city balked at the court judgment, which was partially overturned in the 1970s, and didn't have the funds to build the demanded houses. But after forty years or so of fitful starts and countless disappointments, the city and government agencies tired of the disgraceful saga and reached an agreement to build the housing required. That dragged on for more years, but actual progress was made, closing in on finally ending the case. How many were hurt along the way cannot be measured, but nothing in Hamtramck's history began with such promise and delivered such failure.

Urban renewal took on a whole new meaning in Hamtramck as the bitter case dragged on and on. But it was very much a reflection of the tumultuous 1960s and especially 1968, which was seared in the minds of many as the worst year in modern American history.

EXPERIENCE IT

Go to Wyandotte Street, east of Lumpkin Street, and face west. This was the heart of the urban renewal project. Give a hard look at the mix of houses and industry in the area.

In the News

Court Ruling to Cost City $1.8 Million for Pensions

The Common Council was informed Tuesday that the State Court of Appeals has ruled in favor of police and fire department retirees seeking back pension benefits from the city that could cost Hamtramck $1,800,000.
— The Citizen, *March 21*

Air Pollution Control Device to Be Installed at Chevrolet Gear Plant Here

Two high-volume air pollution control devices are being installed at the power house shared by Chevrolet's Detroit Gear & Axle and Forge plants. Richard C. Walter, manager of the Hamtramck manufacturing complex, said the two electrostatic precipitators are designed to catch and retain virtually all dust and flying ash from the coal-burning furnaces at the power house.
— The Citizen, *June 20*

School Board Raises Teachers $900–$1,000 in New Agreement

The Hamtramck Board of Education approved a new teacher contract that raises beginning salaries $900 above the current $6,100 per year, and top salaries to $12,000, up from the current top of $12,000.
— The Citizen, *August 15*

Muskie Comes to Hamtramck

Senator Edmund S. Muskie, democratic nominee for the vice presidency, will be in Hamtramck Wednesday to deliver a major address at a street rally at Jos. Campau and Caniff. This will be the Maine senator's first trip to Michigan since his nomination August 29 in Chicago.
— The Citizen, *September 26*

9

1987

Pope John Paul II climbed the steps of the huge stage erected at the giant empty lot that was being converted into the Hamtramck Town Center shopping mall. He surveyed the crowd, which wasn't as large as one would expect to greet a Polish pope in a mainly Polish community, but that did not dampen his enthusiasm. Nor did the early morning rain that arrived before he did.

"In the course of my lengthy papal pilgrimage to the church of the United States, God has led me to Detroit, the second-largest community of people of Polish origin after Chicago. And here I am in Hamtramck, the city I know very well," the pope told a delighted audience. He went on to speak of the cultural heritage he shared with the Polish people here and praised the local Ukrainians as well. "I bless the sons and daughters of Saint Vladimir and Saint Olga, as well as all the faithful of the Church in the Ukraine and abroad."

It wasn't a long presentation, about a half hour, but it did resonate with the listeners. For some, it was a landmark moment in their lives. After all, how often does one get to see a pope in person? The moment culminated months of planning on an international scale. John Paul II was the most traveled of all popes, eventually visiting 129 countries and covering an estimated 750,000 miles.

In early 1987, it was announced that Pope John Paul II would come to the United States, and as part of his tour, he would stop at Detroit and deliver a speech in Hamtramck. John Paul's original name was Karol Wojtyla, and he had a personal connection to Hamtramck. His cousin John Wojtylo had been on the common council in the 1940s and '50s. In early 1987,

A light rain coated the area before the pope arrived. That didn't stop people from lining the streets, under umbrellas.

Hamtramck residents were issued parking passes for the day Pope John Paul II was to arrive in Hamtramck. But the anticipated parking crunch never materialized.

the archdiocese announced that the pope would come to Hamtramck in September. At that time, the city still had a fairly substantial Polish population, and the announcement of his visit electrified the town. Just a few years earlier, the city had led the effort to establish Pope Park, a one-lot corner park on Jos. Campau Avenue at Belmont Street. Its centerpiece is a large statue of the pope on a high pedestal. The announcement that the pope would actually see that statue was thrilling to many people. It was as if a lost son was coming home, although he wasn't lost and he wasn't from here.

But the pope was not a newcomer to Hamtramck. As archbishop of Krakow, Poland, he first came to Hamtramck in September 1969 and visited at St. Florian Church.

In 1987, Hamtramck was in a transition stage, although no one realized it at the time. Jos. Campau Avenue was slipping in its status as a bustling shopping district. Many of the key retailers, like the Federal's Department Store, had closed. All the theaters were gone. In fact, the decayed hulk of the old Conant Theatre, which had been closed since the 1950s, was demolished in August. It wasn't the only historical building the city would lose that year. The venerable Strickland Funeral Home on Mitchell Street was torn down, and a fire destroyed the Dodge Local 3 hall on Jos. Campau. The latter building was tied to the long history of the Dodge Main factory, which had been demolished six years earlier. The popular Balkan Village restaurant on Jos. Campau Avenue also was a victim of fire and joined the demolition roster. Vacant lots on main streets were increasing, and Hamtramck was beginning to look a bit ragged. Mayor Robert Kozaren identified one hundred decrepit, abandoned houses in the city that needed to be torn down. However, identifying how to pay for the demolitions proved to be more challenging.

Beyond the physical appearance, the character of Hamtramck was slowly changing. It still was primarily a Polish community, but new immigrants were starting to move into town. Albanians, Chaldeans and, to a lesser extent, Yemenis and Bangladeshis were making the city their home. They would not have a greater impact for another decade, but the pattern had been set, yet few realized that in the 1980s.

And the Polish character was brought into focus with the planned visit of the Polish pope.

On March 1, nearly one hundred journalists toured the city to get a feel of what to expect when the pope arrived. At a lunch that day at the Polish American Century Club on Holbrook Street, it was announced that Father Ted Blaszczyk, the popular pastor of Our Lady Queen of Apostles Church, had been named as leader of the welcoming committee to handle plans for the pope's visit.

"We have to portray this not as a circus but a pastoral visit," Father Blaszczyk later said. "The pope is the pastor of his church and it's his responsibility to visit his flock." But this was not a mere visit. This was an event of monumental proportions—literally. It was quickly decided that the pope would deliver his address to the community from a specially constructed stage that resembled a rather large building. It was to be erected at the planned shopping center site that at this point wasn't much more than a huge dusty lot. It required the services of an architect provided by the archdiocese and input from the journalist contingent who would recommend how the stage should be oriented for the best access for the cameras and crowd. And then there was the issue of security. This was a critical consideration because the pope already had been wounded in an assassination attempt in May 1981 in Vatican City. James G. Huse Jr., special agent in charge of security for the U.S. Secret Service, which was coordinating security for the visit, said that there had been five attempts to assassinate him. Secret Service agents began to visit the city as soon as the visit was announced to check out the site and meet with local officials. "We have to be mindful of everything that goes on," Huse said. He warned that residents should expect to be inconvenienced during the visit. Barriers were going to be erected in certain areas, and parking would be limited. Some streets would be blocked, and others would temporarily be made into emergency routes. All of this was designed to provide maximum protection for the pope, and in case of an emergency, security officers could respond instantly and effectively. "No one should really be outraged," he said. "But some aspects of daily life in Hamtramck will be changed. It's not going to be an everyday Saturday."

That quickly ended the hope of having the pope stop at Pope Park. There was a four-story building directly across the street, which security officials said would be difficult to secure. Instead, the pope would drive down Jos. Campau Avenue in the famous "Popemobile" from the north side of town directly to the speaking site.

The pope cruised down Jos. Campau Avenue in his famous Popemobile.

In fact, security would have a major effect on the whole event, going well beyond what anyone had anticipated. Parking was going to be restricted the day of the visit. Even entering the city was going to be a challenge, or so it was thought at the time.

Thousands of people were expected to attend the event, with many coming from outside of Hamtramck. Portable toilets would be needed, and a major sound system would have to be installed so all could hear him.

"Thousands of people will come to Hamtramck to see the holy father," Father Blaszczyk said. "We have to respect who they are and go out of our way to extend a helping hand. They might camp overnight. We have to provide for their needs."

By July, plans for the visit were well underway. The city had solicited volunteers—and more than one hundred people responded—to help with the setup of traffic barriers, staff first-aid stations, give visitors directions and clean up after the event.

"I've never been involved in anything that takes this much planning," said police lieutenant Arnold Morosky, who was coordinating traffic and crowd control. At a series of planning meetings, the police and Secret Service identified routes and street closings and determined where two first-aid stations would be located along the path of the Popemobile. They decided there would be two first-aid stations at the site where the pope would speak, one at Holbrook and Brombach Streets and one at Wyandotte and Lumpkin

Streets. Both were in easy walking distance of the site. Security officers were to be stationed around the area. People were told they could bring cameras and binoculars, but they had to be clearly visible to security officers. All bags would be checked. Residents were also told to do their shopping and run errands in the days before the visit because maneuvering through town on that Saturday was going to be a challenge. An estimated 100,000 people were expected to cram into Hamtramck. "Try to sit tight that day," Morosky said.

While much of the planning resembled strategizing a military operation, there were lighter moments. In late July, Mayor Robert Kozaren joined with Warren mayor Ronald Bonkowski, Dearborn mayor Michael Guido, Kowalski Sausage Company president Ron Kowalski and several other music makers to provide backup vocals to the "VIP Polka," which had been written and was being recorded by the Gaylords. That duo of Ronnie Gaylord and Burt Holliday had been especially popular in the metro Detroit area, although they did achieve some nationwide attention, especially in Las Vegas. That wasn't the only song inspired by the pope. Hamtramckan Leon Zarski, who had won two Grammy Awards for his polkas, penned "Our Pope, Our Shepherd," which was performed by Carol Gajac-Topoldki at the city's annual Labor Day festival just prior to the pope's visit. Sales of the record were used for a plaque at Pope Park. As if those melodic tributes weren't enough, "The Pope Is Here in the U.S.A.," written and performed by Giacomo Carmicino of Shelby Township, didn't make the charts, but it did get play on local radio stations.

Final plans were settling into place by the first week of September, and a sense of seriousness was evident. The police issued stern warnings that persons parking illegally during the visit would have their vehicles towed. Additional tow trucks had been brought in to enforce the parking ban. The people were advised that barricades were going to be erected on streets along the papal route beginning on Monday, September 14, but wouldn't interfere with traffic immediately. But beginning Thursday morning, parking would be banned on Jos. Campau until the Monday after the visit.

On Friday, September 18, all the pieces were in place. Designated streets had been blocked off; parking and traffic were restricted. Residents had been given passes to access the streets in front of their homes, routes for shuttle buses from areas around Hamtramck were designated and construction of the massive stage where the pope was to speak was done. It had become somewhat of a tradition for large stages to be built for papal visits around the world, and this would hold true in Hamtramck. The stage measured 120 feet by 77 feet and had seating for sixty bishops, a choir and musicians.

As had become the custom, a huge stage was erected for the pope to speak from at a large lot at the corner of Holbrook and Jos. Campau Avenues. It was large enough to hold an orchestra and a Polish dancing troupe.

That included the archdiocesan papal choir and the sixty-two-member Hamtramck Concert Band.

Stores planned to be open all night, and vending trucks with enough food to feed thousands of people were in place to restock the stores as needed. An air of excitement had built throughout the week. The papal visit was big news in Hamtramck for months, but now everything was actually happening.

"It was a very exciting time," said Joan Bittner. She and her husband, Ray, own the popular Polish Art Center on Jos. Campau Avenue, just a few blocks from the site where the pope was to speak. They specialize in Polish imports, including Polish pottery and amber. But their focus at this time was on Pope John Paul memorabilia. And people were buying. "They all came to Hamtramck for souvenirs," Joan said. The Bittners covered the counters that contained the usual merchandise with special displays of papal material—key chains, paper fans, plates with the pope's image—whatever would serve as a reminder of this special occasion. "Anything pope related was hot," Ray said. It made for a busy day and night. Joan remembers catching some sleep on boxes containing jars of pickles in the back room as customers came in at 3:00 a.m.

While there were people on the streets all through the night, by 1:00 a.m. most were gone, and stores, which had planned to be open all night, closed.

Joan and Ray Bittner operate the Polish Art Center on Jos. Campau Avenue, which specializes in Polish imports. Their business drew customers throughout the night of the pope's visit.

St. Florian Church, two blocks north of the staging area, was bedecked with a large banner welcoming the pope. The church is a majestic Gothic masterpiece of architecture dominated by a lofty nave. It exudes grandeur yet is a tranquil place—especially when no one is there. And that almost was the case the night before the pope's visit. It was thought that people would want to see the church that the pope had visited nineteen years earlier. But few did.

"We expected people to come in the night [before]," said Cindy Cervenak, a lifelong member of the parish and a volunteer who spent the night at the church to guide visitors. But while a few people came early in the morning, "It was not as crazy as everyone expected it to be," Cervenak said. Even so, "It was a memorable occasion. It was a very moving occasion."

When the morning came, so did the rain, but it wasn't harsh, and residents began to congregate along Jos. Campau leading toward the stage site. Families and individuals clustered under umbrellas as they sat on the curb of Jos. Campau Avenue. Some brought binoculars, which they trained on the street looking north—the direction the Popemobile was to come from. At the papal staging area, a crowd assembled, some having spent the night there. But it was hardly what had been expected. Despite great attendance expectations, the actual number was far below what was anticipated. It was

When the pope arrived at the speaking site, he passed through the crowd, personally greeting many people.

easy to drive down the streets, although so many were blocked that the local folks just walked to the center of town. When the Popemobile was finally spotted, it raced down Jos. Campau so quickly it was difficult for people to snap a quick photo. Still some people managed to throw carnations on the street in front of the Popemobile.

The pope did not disappoint in his arrival at the stage. He greeted people in the crowd, touching their hands as he moved up to the platform where he delivered his address. A benefit of the sparse crowd was that those who did come were able to get close to the stage and get a good view of the pope. Why was the crowd so thin? Afterward it was speculated that there had been so much publicity about the tight security, the closing of streets and limited parking that a lot of people were just scared off and opted to go to the other metro area sites where the pope was appearing that day. It was just easier to get in and out there, it was assumed.

Although the vendors who planned to sell refreshments to big crowds were stuck with a large amount of unsold goods, for the average person it was a day to remember. Even non-Christians could appreciate the significance of having a world leader of that stature coming to town.

The pope spoke. People listened. And then he was gone. Back aboard the Popemobile he sped off to Detroit. People lingered in town the rest of the day and into Sunday. In the days that followed, the streets were reopened, the banners lowered and the huge stage dismantled. Life returned to normal. In a way, it was anticlimactic. After so many months of planning, it was over so quickly. Some found relief in that. The pope's visit to Hamtramck had been successful. Nothing went seriously wrong, and the city shone brightly on the international stage.

"It was a good time," Ray Bittner remembered.

EXPERIENCE IT

Pope John Paul II stands tall over Pope Park at the corner of Belmont Street and Jos. Campau. A large statue of the pope lords over the small park. A second memorial is at the Hamtramck Town Center. It is a miniature re-creation of the stage the pope stood on.

In the News

Arsonist Burns Dodge Local 3 Union Hall

Hamtramck and Highland Park firefighters battled a blaze Sunday on the city's south side that destroyed a landmark and marked the third major arson-related fire in the past three weeks in that area. Firefighters spent over four hours extinguishing a fire at the vacant UAW Dodge Local 3 hall at Jos. Campau and Alice.

—The Citizen, *January 22*

Zarski Comes Back Home with a Grammy Award

Hamtramck's newest celebrity, Grammy award winning song writer Leon Zarski, returned to Hamtramck after spending six days in Los Angeles where he was co-winner of Polka of the Year honors. Zarski, and his wife, Carol, wrote the polka I Remember Warsaw, *which was recorded by the Jimmy Sturr band.*

—The Citizen, *March 5*

"Tip" Delights Crow at Mayor's Fund Raiser

Despite a sparse turnout, retired speaker of the U.S. House of Representatives, Thomas "Tip" O'Neal, delighted the crowd at Mayor Robert Kozaren's Friday fundraiser with firm handshakes, jokes and jabs at the Reagan administration.

—The Citizen, *July 2*

Test Scores Show HHS Students Are Better Readers

Last year, only 38 percent of the tenth graders in Hamtramck High School said they read in their spare time. This year, the number rose to 60 percent, and tenth grade scores in the Michigan Educational Assessment Program (MEAP) test rose from 58.3 percent to 78.6 percent.

—The Citizen, *November 19*

10

1997

Alex took a few steps back from the front window, unsure of just what was happening and what to do. And for the first time in his life, he felt genuine fear. Fear for his life.

The day had been blisteringly hot and sticky. It had an odd feel to it, unlike a typical hot summer day. The humidity seemed exceptionally high, and the temperature was extreme. Storms were predicted, so when the clouds moved in, no one was surprised. In fact, a storm might have brought some relief from the sticky heat. But at about 6:15 p.m. on Wednesday, July 2, the sky suddenly grew dark, very dark, and the wind erupted with a howling force. Alex had been sitting on the couch watching TV. He had just gotten home from work and parked his car across from the two-story house where he lived on Mitchell Street, just north of Holbrook Avenue. He lived in the upper flat, which was perfectly suited for his lifestyle. It was neat and comfortable, with the only problem being parking. The street was always crowded, so he had to look for a place to park every day when he returned from work in the suburbs. But that was just a fact of life in Hamtramck. After a quick supper, he had plopped down on the couch and turned on the TV. He was looking forward to the upcoming long holiday weekend and was thinking about what he was going to do.

He didn't pay much attention to the thickening clouds and when it started to rain. But rapidly, the rain turned into a rush of wind and water. Then there was a huge snap, and something smashed into the front of the house. He jumped up and looked out the front window. All he could see at first was

The view from Alex's front porch after the tornado passed nearby, uprooting trees along its path.

a gigantic mass of leaves covering the entire window. Then they slipped to the side, revealing more, and he realized that it wasn't just a tree branch that had broken and smashed into the house—it was the entire tree. A tree that was taller than the house and had been pulled out of the ground. But now it was hardly more than an oversized twig blowing in the wind. Alex backed away from the window a bit, unsure whether it was going to shatter. That's when the fear began to set in. For as he stood there in the living room, the entire house began to sway from side to side. Slowly and gently, but he definitely could feel the motion. It was something he had never experienced before in a house. And that's when he thought, "I better get out of here." He turned and rushed to the back door leading to the stairs. But as suddenly as the motion started, it stopped. The now howling wind quieted, and the sky lightened. He knew something big and bad had just happened, and it might have been a tornado. But he had lived his life of nearly fifty years in Hamtramck, and in that span, the city had never experienced a tornado, at least that he knew of.

His courage returning, Alex went back to the front window and looked out. There was no question that the city had been hit by a tornado and hit hard. The street was littered with trees that had fallen down or been entirely uprooted and tossed across the road and sidewalks. His car had narrowly avoided being crushed by a massive tree, but his neighbor hadn't been as lucky. His car lay flattened under a tree trunk. Huge chunks of sidewalks had been ripped up. But none of the houses appeared severely damaged.

The TV was off. A quick check of the lights showed that there was no power in the house, which was hardly surprising. Looking out the back door, Alex saw the utility poles in the alley had been knocked over; some were snapped in half and hanging by the wires they were supposed to support.

The sky started to clear, and Alex went outside. The scene was shocking. All down the block, trees were lying across the road. Many cars were crushed. Some neighbors were coming out to inspect the damage. It struck Alex that the biggest threat they were facing was fire. Electrical wires were down everywhere, and the streets were completely blocked to traffic. A fire truck could not get near a burning building.

There was nothing that Alex could do there, so he set out to see how extensive the damage was. Jos. Campau Avenue was only a block away, and what he saw when he turned the corner onto it was surreal. Damage was widespread. Many buildings along Jos. Campau had been stripped of their façades, sometimes revealing beautiful brickwork that had been

The tree in front of the house where Alex lived was torn out of the ground and thrown onto the porch. Alex rented the second-story flat.

added over the years to modernize the look of the buildings. There were piles of rubble in the street. Adding to the eeriness of the scene was the near total silence. Jos. Campau was usually a busy street, but this time it was tomblike. Alex didn't realize it then, but he actually had been walking away from the worst of the storm's damage. Conant Avenue, which was the counterpart of Jos. Campau but farther east, had been pounded by the passing tornado, which had basically traveled along the length of the street from Carpenter Street at the city's northern border to Holbrook Avenue about half a mile south before taking an abrupt turn east and roaring into Detroit. Along the way, it demolished completely or severely damaged dozens of buildings. The venerable Kanas Hall building at the corner of Conant and Evaline had its front almost completely ripped off by the storm. It would later be demolished. The Allen Lumber Company at the intersection of Holbrook and Conant Avenues was obliterated. It was gone for good. The Knights of Columbus hall, just north of the lumberyard, also was severely damaged but would be rebuilt. A two-story house on Conant Avenue was split open along its side, and the furniture was exposed as the pieces clung to the remains of the wall. That scene was repeated all down the street.

Soon emergency vehicles were on the scene, as much as possible, to seal off the main streets where the damage had been most severe. Media began to arrive to cover the breaking story, and they certainly had the opportunity for some memorable graphics. It looked like the city had been bombed, but the storm was indeed a tornado. It had originated in the west side of Detroit, traveled east through Highland Park and followed Carpenter Street through Hamtramck to Conant Avenue, then turned south along Conant to Holbrook and then went back into Detroit and through to the Grosse Pointes, finally dissipating over Lake St. Clair. The National Weather Service later said the storm had winds of 180 miles per hour. Along its path, it tore the roofs off of houses, scoured the front and sides from buildings and carried debris across a wide area. Alex walked along the length of Jos. Campau to Carpenter, taking in the sight of all the damage. More people were coming outside and already had begun the cleanup process. Saws and other tools were being used to cut tree limbs, although it would take heavy equipment to move the stumps and chunks of sidewalks. People were in somewhat of a daze as they worked. As night approached, Alex returned home. He brought out an old radio he had and found some batteries. This at least put him back in touch with the outside world. The story of the storm was being carried everywhere. He learned

Many buildings were severely damaged, some torn to pieces. Cars were upturned and crushed.

that Hamtramck had been hit the hardest by the storm, but miraculously no one in the city had been killed—although a resident did die later of a heart attack while cleaning up the debris.

As the sun set, it grew darker than it had in more than a century in Hamtramck. There were no streetlights through much of the area. Buildings and homes were dark, and it would not be an exaggeration to say that that night was perhaps the most uncomfortable in the history of Hamtramck. It was hot, almost no one had any air conditioning or even fans and there was still the shock of what just happened. A great silence settled over the city that was interrupted, ironically, only by the gentle wind.

In the morning the rescue forces had assembled and were coming to the area. Utility crews from across the Midwest were arriving or on their way. This was not going to be a simple rewiring project. Poles carrying telephone and electrical wires were shattered and had to be uprooted and replaced by new poles. Trucks with lifts and heavy equipment and saws were busy cutting up branches and stumps and removing shattered and uprooted pieces of sidewalk concrete. But most of the cars were going to be trapped for at least a few days as the roads were cleared. And it wouldn't be until the following week that power was restored.

Buildings collapsed and/or had their roofs torn away. Debris littered the streets. It looked like a war zone.

Almost immediately, neighboring communities were sending police and cleanup crews to help restore a sense of order. The Red Cross was in town by the next day to offer assistance. The city implemented a 10:00 p.m. curfew for safety, but there were no reports of looting or serious disorderly conduct. Trash pickups were restored in a few days. The city also issued an advisory to residents to check with the city's building department before hiring any contractors to do repairs on damaged homes and buildings. The city would provide a list of licensed contractors who would do proper repairs. And homeowners could qualify for assistance from the Federal Emergency Management Agency. Among the most damaged sites was Dickinson Elementary School, which fortunately had been empty when the tornado hit, smashing into the west side of the building between Edwin and Norwalk Streets. The gym and several classrooms were especially hit hard.

"People are shocked, upset and confused by these events," said Elizabeth DeWalls, president of the Dickinson East Elementary Parent Association. "We want to make sure that everybody is OK and that the building will be safe once it is rebuilt."

Michigan governor John Engler, Detroit mayor Dennis Archer, U.S. senators Carl Levin and Spencer Abraham and U.S. representative Carolyn Cheeks-Kilpatrick visited the city, which had been declared an official disaster area.

Hamtramck mayor Robert Kozaren issued a statement to the community offering encouragement as the rebuilding process began.

"Less than an hour after the most devastating storm in Hamtramck's history, our residents, public servants and friends banded together behind a common cause. Our goal, though never spoken, was a simple one: To restore peace and tranquility to our neighborhoods and to our hometown." He went on to thank the residents for their reasoned response to the disaster.

"Above all, I want everyone to know how proud I am of our entire community. Years from now we will reminisce about this experience. I say that what we will remember most is the way our community came together. Neighbors helping neighbors. Our brother and sister cities coming to our aid."

Within a few days, most streets were cleared, and residents were allowed to move around again. Stores reopened, and a sense of normalcy returned. Alex was able to go back to work by the following Monday, and life went on as before. But the community was never quite the same. The damaged buildings were all repaired or demolished. But the city had lost hundreds of trees, some many decades old. What had been shady streets became

Cleanup began shortly after the storm passed. Mounds of rubble blocked the streets.

somewhat exposed. Over the years, various tree planting programs would restore many of those that were lost.

As a postscript, it's interesting to note that this may not have been the first and only tornado in Hamtramck history. In August 1939, a brief but intense storm hit, causing some localized damage on the north side of the city. According to an article in *The Citizen* newspaper, the storm struck at 4:30 p.m. "The first notice I had that the wind was acting up was when a window on the north side of the room let go with a bang," said Ted Piechoecinski, proprietor of a bar at 3141 Caniff Street that felt the brunt of the storm. "The wind howled through the room, sweeping all of the glasses off the bar and stacking the chairs in the middle of the floor. Then a south window blew into the street. A second later the wind, evidently circling the corner, smashed in the east window. When I got to the door the wind had died down."

The storm then shot toward the northeast, past Gallagher, Sobieski, Klinger and Moran Streets. Piechoecinski's bar wasn't the only place damaged. A six-foot-tall wooden fence across the street from Piechoecinski's bar was smashed to pieces, which were carried away and landed on the roof of Copernicus Junior High School, where a number of windows were broken.

Two large trees in front of Ernest Rybarski's house at 11643 Moran were uprooted, forcing a closing of the street. "I never saw anything like it," Rybarski said. "It got as dark as night, and when I looked out of the window, I could see bits of wreckage flying in a circular manner. It was a cyclone, sure enough."

According to residents who saw the storm, its path "was no more than 100 feet wide and was not felt on streets a block away on either side of its course."

That matched the description of a small tornado, but there was no weather service at that time that could measure or even detect such a small, specific storm. There have been plenty of storms in Hamtramck since then, but nothing has matched the ferocity of the one on that steamy evening in July 1997.

EXPERIENCE IT

You can't, unless you stand in the path of a tornado. That is not recommended.

The venerable Kanas Hall on Conant Avenue felt the full force of the storm and was torn apart. What was left was later demolished.

IN THE NEWS

DDA TAX PLAN TO ADDRESS PARKING

The Hamtramck Downton Development Authority is nearly ready to ask the common council to approve a 2-mill tax on all properties on Campau for the next 15 years….Money collected from the tax will be used to alleviate the parking crunch in town.

—The Citizen, *January 23*

"DISNEYLAND" JUST KEEPS GROWING

Folk artist Dmytro Szylak continues to add on to his whirligig set in his Klinger St. yard. With warmer weather here, flocks of visitors are again coming by to crane their necks and admire the overhead web of creation.

—The Citizen, *June 5*

IT'S THE LAST STITCH FOR CLOTHING STORE

For about 50 years Witkowski Clothes for Men provided some of the finest threads in town. But with the era of dressing up in suits exchanged for a time of dressing down in the work place, well, it's been a tough sell lately to be in the suit business. So chalk another longtime business in Hamtramck that's closing the cash register for the last time.

—The Citizen, *October 30*

ZYCH STILL ON TOP

The counting is over. Mayor-elect Gary Zych will serve as the city's next Mayor Come Jan. 1. That's the official word following last Tuesday's tense and often emotional recount of the mayoral election, which was requested by Mayor Robert Kozaren who was turned out of office by nine votes.

—The Citizen, *December 11*

Conclusion

TODAY

I step into the rain.
    I don't care that it's raining. We're going for a walk. The best way to see a town is from the sidewalk level, and there are plenty of sidewalks in various states of condition in Hamtramck. Our starting point is Moran Street, at the north side of town. Despite its location, it is one of the oldest streets in town. I say "despite its location" because Hamtramck generally grew from the south to the north, developing farms into streets with homes and businesses. But even as much of the surrounding area was farmland, Moran Street was established. It was named after Charles Moran, the supervisor of Hamtramck Township back in 1820s. He wouldn't recognize the place today. Like almost all of Hamtramck, it was divided into thirty-foot-wide lots. It's a mix of single- and multiple-family houses, all of which have undergone some degree of renovations over the years. Heading south at the corner of Moran and Casmere Streets is what used to be a corner store. Stores like this once populated seemingly every second corner of the city. Stores and, of course, bars.

This store didn't stand out from the others scattered about except that in 1929 someone drove a car into the building. No one was hurt, but the building took a good hit. The scars are healed, and while the building still resembles a store, it no longer is one. Now it's another house in the row that stretches up and down the block. Across Casmere, the line of houses stands unbroken. The set of six closest to the intersection are clearly newer constructions than most of the houses found around the city. All are

In October 1929, a car plowed into the Kazdiol confectionery at the corner of Moran and Casmere Streets. The store was later converted into living space, but it retains some features of a store.

constructed of brick, which would have been too expensive for the earlier immigrants who settled in the city mainly after 1910. But the other side of the street is more typical of the Hamtramck housing stock. These are the multifamily units that provided the space for the monumental influx of immigrants who came here for the jobs the numerous factories operating then offered. Perhaps these houses were built by Albert Gorlaczyk, a contractor who helped erect hundreds of houses in the city after 1910. An immigrant from Poland, he came to the United States in 1897 and moved to Hamtramck in 1910. He died in 1937 and was buried in Mt. Olivet Cemetery, the final resting place of many Hamtramckans.

At the corner of Caniff Street, we have to make a choice—go left to Conant Avenue or right toward Jos. Campau Street. This time, we're going into the rising sun although it's still overcast, so we head toward Conant. On our left is a strip mall of recent origin. For years, this was the location of the Conant-Caniff market. It was a step above the corner store but not of the level of the Pure Food markets that were on Jos. Campau Avenue. Sadly, the Conant-Caniff market burned down some years ago, but at least the space is still productive. At Conant Avenue, we make a right and head south. This is Hamtramck's second shopping district. It runs along the city's eastern

Hamtramck streets are tight. Most houses are built on lots thirty feet wide by one hundred feet deep. Yet the houses show a lot of character.

edge through the entire town and into Detroit. It's one of the oldest roads in Hamtramck and was named for Shubael Conant, a nineteenth-century landowner and abolitionist. Just north of Hamtramck lies Conant Gardens, a neighborhood of Detroit named in his honor. It was one of the few places in the Detroit metro area where Black people were allowed to buy property and have decent housing for many years. But back to Hamtramck: Conant Avenue street signs also carry the alternate name of Bangladesh Avenue. The street received the honorary title in recognition of the number of businesses owned by Bangladeshi immigrants. Here can be found restaurants, food markets (some selling live chickens), clothing stores featuring fascinating examples of ethnic clothes, travel agencies, driving schools and such. The mix reflects the needs and interests of the new immigrant population. Here can be found Aladdin Sweets and Café, the "home of authentic Bangladeshi food and dessert." Down the street is the Kabob House, the former Orlikowski Funeral Home, which has been converted into a Bangladeshi restaurant. There's also Boniful Sweets and Café not far from the Bengal Auto Sales. But the transformation isn't complete. Small's club at the corner of Conant Avenue and Caniff Street still hosts some of the best rock bands around.

Because of the growing number of businesses owned by Bangladeshi immigrants, Conant Avenue in Hamtramck has been given the honorary title of Bangladesh Avenue.

Hookah lounges are appearing regularly around town. Barbershops or, rather, salons also are more popular than ever.

Times change. What once was the Polish American Century Club is now an ethnic food market.

Speaking of cultural blends, Al-Qamar Pizza and Subs offers a tasteful treat. Like Amar Pizza on the other side of town, the fare offered there is not defined by geography or culture. Halal pizza is terrific.

Walking down the street, I hear many voices, but most are speaking foreign languages. And it seems like every second person I pass is talking into a cellphone. But I also notice how many people say "Hello" to me and smile. They seem to want to make a friendly impression and are extremely polite. When I reach Holbrook Avenue, I make a right turn to head west. Here is a blend of businesses and houses. Until about 1905, a large creek at the bottom of a ravine flowed along this route. There is no indication of it now. But ironically, the sidewalk along this area is about two feet above the level of the street, and there is a steep concrete incline between the street and sidewalk that makes walking there a bit treacherous, especially in winter. That's exactly what people said about the creek and ravine so many years ago.

That and the name Holbrook are the only links to the past. Holbrook was actually DeWitt C. Holbrook, a Detroit official who owned a large tract of property nearby. Here we also find what used to be the Polish American Century Club, which was a Polish club for decades. With the changing population, it has lost that identity and now is one of the dozens of markets in the city that especially caters to the immigrant population. Not much stands out along this street except the old Polish Legion of American Veterans Hall at the corner of Mitchell Street and Holbrook Avenue. Built in 1925, the impressive brick building sports a large auditorium on the second floor. Over the years, hundreds, perhaps thousands, of political rallies, parties, dances and all sorts of events have been held here. Most recently, it served as a small-scale movie theater and offices of, appropriately, an architect who specializes in historical buildings.

The hall, which used to reek of decades of cigarette smoke, now exudes only history. Founded by Polish veterans in the wake of World War I, the hall was a place they could have a quiet drink even on Sunday since it was a private club. But its most colorful history would be tied into the innumerable political rallies it hosted. In the 1920s and 1930s, political meetings were great social gatherings, with as many as fifteen held a night during election season. Even in the 1990s political rallies were staged there.

From here, I turn right on Mitchell Street and head back north, crossing over to Gallagher Street. As I pass Evaline Street, I can see Hamtramck City Hall to my right a block farther east. This building was constructed in 1927 as Hamtramck Municipal Hospital. Originally operated by the

When Copernicus Junior High School was built in 1931, it was considered one of the most modern schools in the nation. It now serves as Hamtramck High School.

city, it was leased to the Sisters of St. Francis in 1931. They changed it to St. Francis Hospital and operated it until 1969, when it closed and the building was converted to be used as city hall. I, like many Hamtramckans, was born there.

I continue down Gallagher Street, past Caniff Avenue and the last landmark on today's journey: Hamtramck High School.

Or rather, Copernicus Junior High School. That's the title it carried when it opened in 1931. And it was noted as one of the, if not the most, modern schools in America at that time. It had its own radio station studio, a book bindery and print shop and, most notably, a functioning apartment, including kitchen, living room and dining room, where the new immigrant students would learn about home life in America. Hamtramck had perhaps the most progressive education system in the nation thanks mainly to School Superintendent Maurice Keyworth, who attracted national attention for the School Code he largely developed in 1927 that modernized school operations and emphasized teaching immigrant children. Then, as now, the schools were being flooded with new immigrants. Many had special needs, including language problems and physical and mental issues. Keyworth addressed them all. He went on to be elected state school superintendent in 1935 but sadly was killed a short time later in an auto accident. Largely forgotten today, he was a landmark educational figure in his time.

The building stands as a tribute to him. Every time I pass it on my way home, I nod to his memory.

WEDNESDAY

The South End of Hamtramck is intriguing, although it's hard to say why. Perhaps it's the sense of age that weighs so heavily on the buildings here. This is the area of Hamtramck that was settled first, even prior to becoming a village in 1901. The "South End" is an unofficial designation that denotes the area south of Holbrook Avenue to the GM Factory Zero. This is where the Dodge Main plant and Acme Quality Paints were located along with streets like Whiting, Bismark, Newton and Vulcan that are long gone—even though you can still find Vulcan Street on a Google map. It's the oldest part of town. Alice Street runs through here, and more than any other it resembles what Hamtramck was. Here are a few samples of the giant trees that made overhanging arches spanning the street common all across the city until the devastation caused by Dutch elm disease in the 1950s and 1960s. Here also is Holbrook Elementary School, which was Hamtramck's first school dating to the 1890s. If you can tour the inside, you will still see the library with its fireplace and tiled facing. The houses throughout here are a curious mix. Some clearly look like they originally did. A few even have clapboard siding and resisted the tide of renovations that added aluminum siding to so many houses in town during the 1950s. Multifamily homes are common, but there are also bungalows and others that don't fit into any category. All have been remodeled to some degree, but some retain the old wooden porch pillars. Some have undergone dubious renovations, including attempts to enclose what were formerly open front porches. But here, as well as almost every residential street in the city, is a tangible link to the past even though it is of the most tenuous sort. The aroma of cooking fills the air. I'm not sure what it is, but it smells delicious. This is just what you would have smelled decades ago when doors and windows were wide open in the summer. Sometimes you can walk into wave after wave of the aromas, some spicy, some more sedate but all attractive. And just down the street is the Metropolitan Baking Company, which has provided a wonderful counterpoint to the factory odors of the city for decades. The smell of freshly baked bread is ingrained in the

Alice Street is one of the city's oldest streets and, with its overhanging tree branches, still has characteristics of its past.

St. Anne's Community House on Andrus Street provided social services to the immigrant population in the mid-twentieth century.

memory of many area residents who grew up here. Even those who long ago moved to the suburbs fondly remember that delicious scent.

On Andrus Street is the building that served as the St. Anne's Community House for decades. St. Anne's was founded by the Polish Activities League in 1941 and offered a variety of services to help the new immigrants. It operated on a much smaller scale than Tau Beta—the major social agency in town—but filled an important need. St. Anne's ceased operations years ago, but the distinctive building is still in use. This area housed many significant historical buildings, including the old Village Hall and Immaculate Conception Ukrainian Catholic Church along with the old Ukrainian hall on Grayling Street, the Dodge Local 3 hall on Jos. Campau and, of course, Dodge Main, the Acme White Lead Company complex and many other businesses. All are gone, mostly without a trace. But you can stand at the corner of Lumpkin and Alice Streets and look west and south toward Detroit. You will see the upper floors of factories, smokestacks and water towers. Here is where Hamtramck established its persona as an industrial town. There are still some houses standing across the street from the American Axle factory. Heavy industry abutted houses in an uneasy arrangement as Hamtramck developed. The sounds echoing across here at night would have been uncomfortable, at the least. The smells, in sharp contrast to the cooking aromas cited earlier, would have been dangerous. The smokestacks nearby belched who knows what, especially at night. Sometimes neighborhoods were coated with a fine dust in the mornings before air pollution restrictions tightened in the 1960s and 1970s. But in the 1920s, the air in town was so bad the public schools installed special filters to clear the air in the school buildings to protect the kids.

Just around the corner from Denton Street is Clay Street, perhaps the most notorious street in Hamtramck's history. It was here that Paddy McGraw's infamous brothel stood from through the Prohibition era to the mid-1930s. Paddy was one of Hamtramck's most colorful residents. He was well liked for his charity: he sponsored local baseball teams, he took in stray animals and he helped establish the Hamtramck Goodfellows, which still exists to raise money to buy presents for needy children at Christmas. He funded this through the profits of his saloon and brothel that stood next to the railroad tracks. Those tracks brought clients from as far away as Toledo, Ohio, and Bay City, sixty miles north of Hamtramck, to his front door. He breezed through Prohibition but closed in its wake, complaining that there was too much competition when the bars were allowed to reopen. Paddy's building is gone, but across Clay Street is a decaying factory building and next to it is Morrow Street, a large section of which is made of pavement bricks that are still exposed. However, this area is for only the heartiest walkers and is better seen from a car window than on foot.

There is another area of the South End that also has a distinct personality. This is the small portion of Hamtramck on the east side of Conant Avenue south of the viaduct. Christopher, Vincent, Oliver and Miller Streets—actually only a portion of them—are also in Hamtramck but often are overlooked in the big picture of Hamtramck. This is one of the areas where the border between Detroit and Hamtramck intersects, so neighboring houses are in different cities. It's an extremely tight area where streets are narrow. But like so much of the rest of Hamtramck, new immigrants are moving into the area, and a fair amount of renovations and building of new housing is going on. The only historical building is the old Martini (yes, Martini) Lutheran Church dating to about 1914, when Hamtramck's population was mainly German Lutherans. It long ago lost that affiliation and now is a Baptist church. Here too you will find many people wearing traditional Muslim clothes. And what used to be Resurrection Catholic Church just on the Detroit side of the border is an Islamic complex. Scattered through this area are old industrial buildings. Some, like the popular Fowling (a combination of football and bowling) Warehouse, are popular tourist spots. But mostly they are old, empty buildings. Yet they are much more, for these were the workplaces of people who built this town. And their homes nearby witnessed many joyful celebrations and sorrowful tragedies. Children were born there. Many died there. They are our history.

That may be lost on the new immigrant population, as new residents are most concerned with their lives today, not with those who came decades before them. But that attitude is not surprising. Had you met a person a century ago and reminded them that their house was being constructed on what used to be a farm, you most likely would have been met with indifference.

But the more you walk the streets the more you develop a sense of history. You begin to notice details—date stones at the top of buildings, detailed brickwork, names stamped in sidewalks a century ago and especially the architectural details of houses. These all link with the past. You also connect to the present as you meet people. People like to talk to walkers. They say "Hello," often barely even able to utter that in English. But it usually comes with a smile, and that knows no language barrier.

In time, the various populations will move closer together. I notice the language on the street often is English even when spoken by persons who clearly are not from this country. Many people cringe at the thought of Hamtramck no longer being a predominantly Polish community. And that group of immigrants did have the greatest influence on the town, at least since 1910. But all living things evolve. And while Hamtramck "is not what it used to be," neither is anything else. To live is to change.

FRIDAY

Alleys aren't noted for their charm, but in Hamtramck they may have stories of their own to tell. They are long canyons formed by garages, sheds and even barns that once housed horses. They can be eerie; they can be open. And they are still active byways, although mainly as holding areas for trash cans on garbage pickup days. But over the years, they served a variety of purposes—some innocent, some less so. During Prohibition, moonshiners would set up business in the shacks that lined the alleys, placing windows in the back so that drivers could pull up, place their orders and drive away without even getting out of the car. It was like a fast-food drive thru that served liquor. In that same period and even later, the alleys were playgrounds for the neighborhood kids. In fact, a reason the city pushed cleanup programs so much and frequently won awards for its cleanliness was because of concerns the kids playing in the alleys might pick up diseases from the trash. That was when trash was placed in open fifty-five-gallon cans that baked and rotted in the summer sun. The rats had a feast and could overrun an alley. Hunting rats became a form of recreation for kids.

In 1959, the city launched a program to tear down the old barns that were decaying, but it didn't accomplish much. Over the years, there have been attempts to repave the alleys, but the resurfacings have gradually decayed, leaving most to revert to country roads. Longtime residents might remember the scrap collectors who rode horse-drawn wagons through the alleys salvaging whatever they could that might be worth a bit of change. But they fought a losing battle with the increasing number of cars and finally disappeared in the 1960s.

It was on this spot in 1937 that the body of seventeen-year-old Bernice Onisko was found, prompting the biggest murder investigation in the city's history.

Today, however, we are not looking for a nostalgic experience but to get a sense of history in a bitter form. This afternoon I'm walking down the alley between Niebel and Botsford Streets, just east of Mackay Street on the far north end of town. It's a stretch of crumbling pavement and piles of litter that hopefully someday will be picked up. Not far from where the alley runs into Mackay Street there is an unusually stable old barn made out of formed stones. It was here that in March 1937 Hamtramck's most notorious murder was committed. On a Saturday evening, seventeen-year-old Bernice Onisko was grabbed, raped and strangled as she came home from church. She likely was pulled into the alley and ravaged. The next day, a neighbor found her body. The murder horrified the community and set off the largest manhunt in the city's history. Hundreds of tips were followed up by police. None led any further than that decrepit alley. The story was carried on the front pages of newspapers for months. And when it was announced there was a break in the case, it inevitably ended up a dead end. I had seen the photos of the crime scene. During my career as a newspaper reporter, I had seen some pretty grisly sights, but these were truly horrifying. Sadly, her killer was never caught. Most likely, this had been a chance encounter with someone she did not know. These kinds of murders are the most difficult to solve because there is no connection between the killer and the victim except the crime.

Technically, the case is still open, but it is unlikely it will ever be solved. It's difficult to describe the feeling of standing there, the exact spot where the body was found. In a sense, it's touching the past to a degree you can never get by reading an old document or seeing a photo. Yet it's also profoundly sad, even now.

Like time itself, I move on.

SATURDAY

If a street can define a city, Jos. Campau Avenue is Hamtramck. Since township days, Jos. Campau has been the main street of Hamtramck in every way. The earliest settlers in this area clustered alongside Jos. Campau. When the Dodge brothers selected a site to build their factory in 1909, they picked a lot alongside Jos. Campau. As more businesses opened, most located on Jos. Campau. And Hamtramck grew northward along Jos. Campau. You can't go where the Dodge Main factory was anymore. It is now part of the huge General Motors Factory Zero complex, but fittingly you can walk the entire length of the street in Hamtramck starting at the railroad tracks at the north edge of Factory Zero. It's fitting because the railroad played such a key role in developing Hamtramck village and city a century and more later. Early on, Jos. Campau was a dirt road with a small mix of houses, stores and saloons. The viaduct was built in 1927 as traffic along Jos. Campau increased and workers on foot who raced to get to the Dodge Main plant just south of the tracks were hopping between cars of moving trains, sometimes with tragic results. Standing under the tracks along the viaduct, you can hear a steady rumble and thumps as the massive cars roll overhead. It feels old. Rising back up to the level of the rest of the street, there are more empty spaces than there should be. Most of the old buildings that occupied this part of the strip are gone, demolished long ago. Village Hall, just to the west, is now a big empty lot that sits across the street from what used to be the ornate Hamtramck State Bank building. It too is gone. But at the corner of Council Street is the venerable set of buildings capped by the date stones inscribed "1912" and "1915." That makes them among the oldest buildings still standing in the city. And the 1915 building was the site of the Jewell Theater in its earliest days. You can still get a sense of the past going by the buildings even though they have been remodeled in recent years.

It doesn't look like much, but the viaduct at Denton Street is a bridge to the past. The rail lines it supports date to the early nineteenth century, and this area was once dominated by factories. Now, the General Motors Factory Zero stands tall on the horizon.

But the sound you hear now is pure today, for the past is interrupted by the Muslim "Call to Prayer," from a mosque located a few blocks north. The wailing sound can be heard five times a day for a few minutes with each presentation. It's a reminder to the faithful to pray and that Hamtramck has changed greatly in recent years. Although, has it really? A century ago, the same statement could have, and surely was, made regarding the Polish immigrants who overwhelmed the town and the original German settlers. One thing about Hamtramck that hasn't changed is its welcoming nature to new residents.

Moving on, we pass Dan Street. It was named after Dan Minock, an early village official. Only a handful of houses are on the street, but that's about all that ever stood there. The street is quite short and dead-ends at the railroad tracks that run up the eastern side of the city. Minock's house still stands, and when he moved in there with his wife in 1913, the dirt street was lined with wooden sidewalks and the streetlight used oil to light the night. Minock served on the village council as village treasurer and held other elected positions. He died in 1947.

There is a story to every street in Hamtramck.

Back on Jos. Campau we pass Alice Street. Look down a short ways, and you can see the weathered red painted bricks of Holbrook Elementary School. It was there in 1900 that the local people decided to create the Village of Hamtramck. Not far ahead is the trendy new coffee shop that opened where the venerable Kopytko meat market stood. Coffee shops and hookah shops—no relation—are becoming increasingly popular in Hamtramck. But there are no franchise coffee shops in Hamtramck; these are all home brews. Looking east again, we come to Veterans Memorial Park. Prior to the creation of Hamtramck Veterans Memorial Park in 1930, Hamtramck had only one meager one-square-block park, variously known as Fairmont Park, Winfield Park and now Zussman Park, that was not suited for much except sitting. After the public school district formed the Recreation Department in 1927, the city finally addressed the need for a proper park. Veterans Memorial Park was in an ideal location—plenty of open space for activities, it had a "natural" barrier on its eastern side formed by the railroad tracks and it abutted Pilsudski School, where Keyworth Stadium was to be built. Veterans Memorial Park ended up having a baseball field where the Negro Baseball League used to play in the days before Major League Baseball was integrated. It is today one of the handful of remaining baseball stadiums where the Negro League played. Across the main field are the smaller diamonds where the 1959 Little League and 1961 Pony League world

Chilean muralist Dasic Fernandez depicted a child, a farmer and a woman in this work inspired by Yemeni culture. The mural is a representation of the largely Yemeni population that lives in the area where the mural is on Jos. Campau Avenue.

champions played. And off to the side are the courts where legendary tennis coach Jean Hoxie trained numerous champions, including Jane "Peaches" Bartkowicz, who won the juniors title at Wimbledon.

Of course, mention must be made of the most distinguished Hamtramck veteran in Hamtramck Veterans Memorial Park—Colonel John Francis Hamtramck. His body was moved from Mt. Elliott Cemetery in Detroit in 1962 and reinterred under the impressive veterans' monument at the front of the park. Stop by and say "Hi." I often do.

Next to the park is the popular Yemen Café, one of dozens of restaurants in Hamtramck, many ethnic, like this. Sheeba restaurant is just steps north of Yemen Café. Yemeni immigrants have concentrated in this part of town, although people of all nations live all across the city. As a reminder, three women pass by with two little kids. They are all wearing full-length burkas, the long gowns that cover their entire bodies and heads. I can see only their eyes. And, most interestingly, the blue flashing shoes that one of the little girls is wearing. That is telling.

I cross Goodson Street. The three-story Scottish Lion Lofts show another evolution of the city. Lofts have become trendy and are attracting another population. Many young people are moving to Hamtramck because they are being priced out of the finer areas of Detroit, where rents have skyrocketed. Hamtramck has become such a popular alternative that it's getting difficult to find a rental here.

I pass more ethnic stores—Bab Alyemen, Al-Noor Supermarket and Hamtramck City Market (its name is printed in Arabic on a red awning above the entrance). Next is New Dodge Bar. This is a wonderful old Prohibition-era bar that even has a tunnel that is visible through a sheet of

The knives look formidable, but the demonstration is purely peaceful. A group of Yemeni men performing traditional Baraa wedding dance at the Hamtramck Town Center.

plastic on the bathroom floor. During Prohibition, the moonshiners could drive a truck into a garage across the alley and move the liquor through the tunnel into the bar. At least, that's the story.

Just ahead to the west side of the street is Hamtramck Town Center, where Pope John Paul II spoke when he visited in 1987 (see chapter 9). The small monument featuring the miniature model of the pope and stage he spoke on are almost lost among the trees alongside a store wall. Back then, the site was still unfinished. Today it is fully occupied. But the historical element here is the distant presence of St. Florian Church. Its steeple rises two hundred feet and dominates the landscape. It was meant to. When it was designed by architect Ralph Adams Cram in the mid-1920s, smokestacks, not steeples, defined the horizon. Cram wanted the great steeple of the church to stand in contrast to the dirty chimneys. He succeeded, but today almost all the chimneys are long gone. Yet you still see the steeple from almost everywhere in the city.

And just below it in my view as I turn into the lot are several men swinging formidable knives, and I believe one has a sword. "Now what?" I think. But I quickly see this is not a fight in progress. In fact, one member of the small group of spectators who stands by tells me that this is a Baraa, a dance that is a tradition of Yemeni weddings. I notice that cars parked nearby are decorated with ribbons. The men make an impressive show, swinging their curved blades as they dance in a circle. Such is the world in Hamtramck today.

"EXCUSE ME, SIR."

A woman is coming up to me as I walk toward the end of the parking lot at the Hamtramck Town Center.

"Can I talk to you for a minute?" she adds before I can barely look at her. She is older but not as old as me, and she looks tired. It is fiercely hot, and I bet she has been out for a while.

"I'm homeless, and I have two kids I'm trying to feed. Do you think you could help a bit?"

Is she telling the truth? I don't know, but I give her a couple of bucks. "I haven't got much," I say. "Thank you," she replies.

When you do a lot of walking, you are bound to meet homeless people, even in the wealthiest communities. But I've only been harassed once while in Detroit and never in Hamtramck. Most people I meet while walking in Hamtramck are super friendly. Sometimes they have long stories, and I can tell they have a lot of issues to deal with, but they mean no harm. And there aren't many.

I walk to the intersection of Jos. Campau and Holbrook Avenue waiting for the light to change. Where I stand at the curb was once the edge of the ravine where Holbrook Creek flowed. Across the street once stood the Dolland farmhouse, which was a local landmark for decades. Looking north, Jos. Campau distinctly narrows for the next one thousand feet or so before widening again. When people talk about Hamtramck's golden age and when they say, "Hamtramck isn't what it used to be" (and they often do), this is really what they are referring to. From the 1920s to the 1960s, the Jos. Campau strip was the second-most popular shopping district in southeast Michigan. Only downtown Detroit did more business than this street in Hamtramck. A host of great stores operated here—Federal's, Neisner's, Kresge's, Witkowski Clothes, Helen's Toyland (every kid's dream), P.C. Jezewski's drugstore (with live leeches), Cunningham's Drug Stores (two—one at each end of the narrow area), Pure Foods (also two, a few blocks apart), Max's Jewelry, Dave Stober's clothing store, Day's

Fashions (still there), The Paris (clothes), the Polish Art Center (also still there), Jeanette's Book Store, Able-Man bookstore (mainly magazines), Respondek Drugs, Campau Clothing, Lendzon's (you would go there to find the thing you couldn't find anywhere else no matter what it was), Delis' and Sweetland's (ice cream), Wonder Bazaar (religious items), New Palace Bakery (oldest business in the city—one-hundred-plus years and still going), Entner's Hardware, Pasttime Theater, Farnum Theater, White Star Theater, Campau Theater and Martha Washington Theater, White Tower Hamburgers, Nichol's Restaurant and literally thousands of other businesses over the years. These days, the variety is much more restricted, and there is still an uncomfortable number of empty storefronts. But in recent years, the city has been making some progress in getting them filled. However, it's not likely Jos. Campau will ever regain its former glory. It's not just a change in the streetscape. People's shopping patterns have shifted, with much more done these days on the internet. Shopping is no longer the social experience it once was.

In the early 1980s, the city adopted the slogan "Hamtramck: A Touch of Europe in America." As the demographic of the town changed, a more appropriate encompassing motto was adopted.

Jos. Campau Avenue has lost much of its bustling action, but it remains a viable shopping district with a distinctive character.

At Caniff Street, Jos. Campau widens appreciably. It isn't clear why the street was given different widths, and we don't know exactly when the change occurred. Records of the early twentieth century are sketchy, but there are references to court cases being brought against the city by landowners who did not want to give up property along Jos. Campau to allow the widening in about 1915. That corresponds to when buildings were being built along Jos. Campau at a quickening pace. And as the auto industry played a greater role in the formation of the village, many of the businesses that opened north of Caniff Street were auto related. Krajenke Buick, Woody Pontiac, Northern Auto Sales, McConnell Chevrolet, Edmund Oldsmobile, Garrity Dodge and other dealerships located there. In addition, there were auto parts suppliers and mechanics located along the strip. It became known as Automobile Row and stretched to Carpenter Avenue in the glory days.

It wasn't all car related, of course. From the late 1930s to the early 1950s, the Bowery nightclub was on Jos. Campau near Carpenter Street. The Bowery was a major venue, drawing some of the top acts in the nation, including Danny Thomas, the Three Stooges, Sophie Tucker, Gypsy Rose

The ghostly ad for Northern Auto Sales is a remnant of when Jos. Campau Avenue north of Caniff Street was known as Automobile Row for the many auto dealerships and supply stores that lined the street.

Lee and others. Old-timers say that Frank Sinatra used to come by, not to perform but to watch the acts. But when owner Frank Barbaro and his wife divorced in the early 1950s, she got the business, and it closed a short time later. The building was later acquired by Woodrow Woody, who owned the Woody Pontiac dealership, and it was torn down. Now it is the parking lot of Woody Plaza, the State of Michigan Department of Human Services building. But look closely at the side of the building to the south of the parking lot, and you can still see the imprint of the roofline of the Bowery.

It's one of the ghosts of old Hamtramck. Look carefully, and you will find them around town. Just a block from the Bowery site is a broken sidewalk that was stamped by contractor Peter Plewa when he put it in place there in the 1920s. It's one of the oldest sidewalks in Hamtramck, but you find his work scattered in spots around the city. In the other direction, you can still find the Northern Auto Sales sign painted on the wall of a building. It dates from the 1930s. At the end of the same block, the Bengal Auto Sales lot with a small building recently opened. And across the street is Mostek Paint and Glass store, one of the oldest businesses in Hamtramck, dating back to 1932. And that is reflective of what Hamtramck is today. A complex mix of old and new people and places. Immigrants of another generation are living and working side by side with new immigrants. They are neighbors and partners, yet separated by language, religion and culture. But if the

The northern border of Hamtramck, looking back into town—and its history.

past predicts the future, this division will fade. It did a century ago when the Polish immigrants moved in, changing the character of the community. Hamtramck evolved into a hybrid of cultures that always maintained a degree of individualism yet came to share a common sense of community. You can see evidence of that happening all through the town today. There are churches and mosques, bars and hookah lounges and neighborhoods where Poles, Yemenis, Bangladeshis, Ukrainians, Filipinos, African Americans and many others live side by side on those compact lots. It's a complex arrangement, but it works so well that it is common for government representatives and journalists from around the world to visit Hamtramck to see how and why it does work so well here.

Standing at Carpenter Avenue, I look across the street into Detroit. There's no physical line between Hamtramck and Detroit here, but there is a distinct difference. You can feel it. Hamtramck is a vibrant community that seems to draw strength from its diversity. I turn back to face Hamtramck and am grateful for what I see and what it is.

EXPERIENCE IT

Go for a walk.

BIBLIOGRAPHY

Assorted copies of *The Citizen*, *Plain Dealer*, *Detroit Tribune*, *Detroit Times*, *Detroit Evening News* cited in text.

Burton, Clarence M. *History of Detroit, 1780 to 1850*. N.p., 1917.

Cahill, Leslie, and John Cornwell, eds. *Our Lady Queen of Apostle Parish 75 Years*. N.p., 1992.

Dunbar, Willis Frederick. *Michigan Through the Centuries*. Vol. 2. New York: Lewis Historical Publishers, 1955.

Farmer, Silas. *The History of Detroit and Michigan*. MA: Higginson Book Company, 1884.

Galster, George. *Driving Detroit: The Quest for Respect in the Motor City*. Philadelphia: University of Pennsylvania Press, 2012.

Georgakas, Dan, and Marvin Surkin. *Detroit: I Do Mind Dying*. Cambridge, MA: South End Press, 1998.

Hamtramck Housing Commission. "First Annual Report." 1940.

Hamtramck Yearbook 1947–1948. Hamtramck, MI: Hamtramck Yearbook Publisher, 1948.

Hyde, Charles, K. *Riding the Roller Coaster: A History of the Chrysler Corporation*. Detroit, MI: Wayne State University Press, 2003.

Inventory of the Municipal Archives of Michigan, No. 82, Wayne County, City of Hamtramck, Preliminary Inventory of Office of Engineer, the Michigan Historical Records Survey, 1940.

Kavieff, Paul. *The Violent Years*. Fort Lee, NJ: Barricade Books, 2001.

Lewis, Ferris E. *Michigan Yesterday and Today*. 7th ed. Hillsdale, MI: Hillsdale Educational Publishers, 1969.

Meier, August, and Elliott M. Rudwick. *Black Detroit and the Rise of the UAW*. New York: Oxford University Press, 1979.

Morris, Bob. *Built in Detroit: A Story of the UAW, a Company, and a Gangster*. Bloomington, IN: Universe LLC, 2013.

Otten, William L., Jr. *Colonel J.F. Hamtramck, His Life and Times*. Vol. 1. Port Arkansas, TX: Published by William L. Otten Jr., 1997.

Palmer, Thomas W. *Detroit in 1837*. Detroit, MI: Burton Abstract & Title Company, 1922.

Plum, Mildred. *History of Tau Beta*. Detroit, MI: Evans-Winter-Heeb, 1938.

The Public School Code of the Hamtramck, Michigan Public Schools, Research Series No. 2, Prepared for the Board of Education, Hamtramck Pubic Schools, Maurice R. Keyworth, 1928.

Radzilowski, Thaddeus. *St. Florian: 75 Years*. N.p., 1983.

Russel, George family, personal correspondence, 1870s, 1880s.

Schramm, Jack E., William H. Henning and Richard R. Andrews. *When Eastern Michigan Rode the Rails*. Glendale, CA: Interurban Press, 1984.

Village of Hamtramck, Minutes of the Meeting of the Village Council, August 29, 1901–July 26, 1905. The Michigan Historical Records Survey Project, 1940.

Village of Hamtramck, Minutes of the Meeting of the Village Council of Hamtramck, 1907–1908. The Michigan Historical Records Survey, 1941.

INDEX

ABOUT THE AUTHOR

Greg Kowalski is a retired journalist who serves as executive director of the Hamtramck Historical Museum. He is also a member of the Hamtramck Historical Commission. A lifelong resident of Hamtramck, he has written eleven books about the city and its colorful history.